I Didn't Know That!

BY TONY TALLARICO

Kidsbooks

Visit us at www.kidsbooks.com

CONTENTS

Strange-But-True Mysteries

THE GIANT STATUES OF EASTER ISLAND

On Easter Sunday in 1722, Dutch Admiral Jacob Roggeveen sailed to a small island in the South Pacific. When he went ashore, he discovered more than 600 giant statues carved from stone, some of which were over 40 feet tall. In 1947, Thor Heyerdahl, a Norwegian archaeologist, led an expedition to try to find out how the statues got there.

LEARN ABOUT THE GIANT STATUES OF EASTER ISLAND
AS YOU LOOK FOR THESE FUN ITEMS:

- ☑ **Artist**
- ❏ **Banana leaves**
- ❏ **Bone**
- ❏ **Carrot**
- ❏ **Drum**
- ❏ **Duck**
- ❏ **Flower**
- ❏ **Flying bat**
- ❏ **Football**
- ❏ **Graduate**
- ❏ **Guitar**
- ❏ **Key**
- ❏ **Ladder**
- ❏ **Mouse**
- ❏ **Owl**
- ❏ **Painted eggs (3)**
- ❏ **Party hats (2)**
- ❏ **Pelican**
- ❏ **Periscope**
- ❏ **Photographer**
- ❏ **Ring**
- ❏ **Rocking chair**
- ❏ **Skateboard**
- ❏ **Stars (3)**
- ❏ **Telescope**
- ❏ **Toucan**
- ❏ **Truck**
- ❏ **Unicorn**
- ❏ **Wagon**
- ❏ **Water bucket**
- ❏ **Witch**

What was used to carve the statues? What was the name of Thor Heyerdahl's craft?

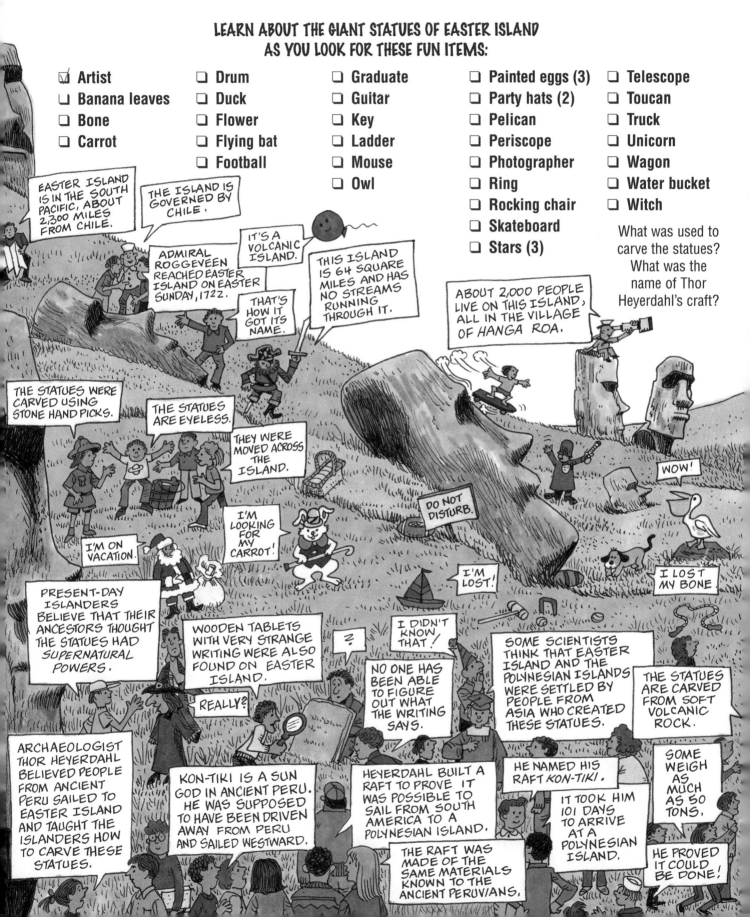

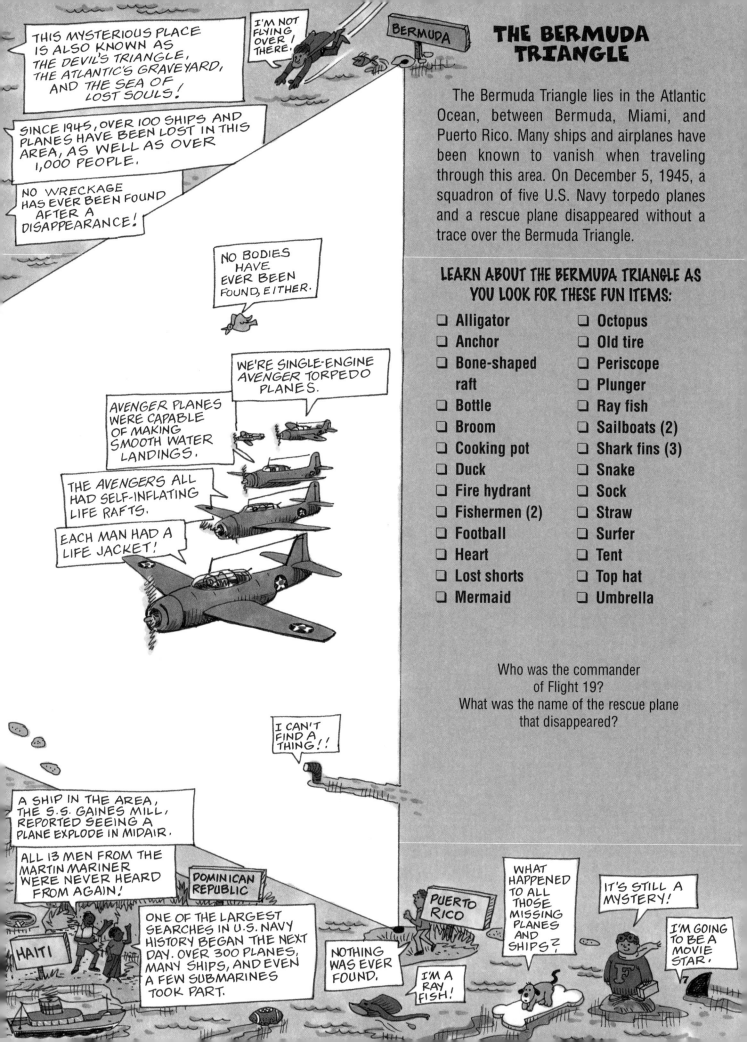

THE BERMUDA TRIANGLE

THIS MYSTERIOUS PLACE IS ALSO KNOWN AS THE DEVIL'S TRIANGLE, THE ATLANTIC'S GRAVEYARD, AND THE SEA OF LOST SOULS!

I'M NOT FLYING OVER THERE.

BERMUDA

SINCE 1945, OVER 100 SHIPS AND PLANES HAVE BEEN LOST IN THIS AREA, AS WELL AS OVER 1,000 PEOPLE.

NO WRECKAGE HAS EVER BEEN FOUND AFTER A DISAPPEARANCE!

The Bermuda Triangle lies in the Atlantic Ocean, between Bermuda, Miami, and Puerto Rico. Many ships and airplanes have been known to vanish when traveling through this area. On December 5, 1945, a squadron of five U.S. Navy torpedo planes and a rescue plane disappeared without a trace over the Bermuda Triangle.

NO BODIES HAVE EVER BEEN FOUND, EITHER.

LEARN ABOUT THE BERMUDA TRIANGLE AS YOU LOOK FOR THESE FUN ITEMS:

- ❑ Alligator
- ❑ Anchor
- ❑ Bone-shaped raft
- ❑ Bottle
- ❑ Broom
- ❑ Cooking pot
- ❑ Duck
- ❑ Fire hydrant
- ❑ Fishermen (2)
- ❑ Football
- ❑ Heart
- ❑ Lost shorts
- ❑ Mermaid
- ❑ Octopus
- ❑ Old tire
- ❑ Periscope
- ❑ Plunger
- ❑ Ray fish
- ❑ Sailboats (2)
- ❑ Shark fins (3)
- ❑ Snake
- ❑ Sock
- ❑ Straw
- ❑ Surfer
- ❑ Tent
- ❑ Top hat
- ❑ Umbrella

WE'RE SINGLE-ENGINE AVENGER TORPEDO PLANES.

AVENGER PLANES WERE CAPABLE OF MAKING SMOOTH WATER LANDINGS.

THE AVENGERS ALL HAD SELF-INFLATING LIFE RAFTS.

EACH MAN HAD A LIFE JACKET!

Who was the commander of Flight 19? What was the name of the rescue plane that disappeared?

I CAN'T FIND A THING!!

A SHIP IN THE AREA, THE S.S. GAINES MILL, REPORTED SEEING A PLANE EXPLODE IN MIDAIR.

ALL 13 MEN FROM THE MARTIN MARINER WERE NEVER HEARD FROM AGAIN!

DOMINICAN REPUBLIC

ONE OF THE LARGEST SEARCHES IN U.S. NAVY HISTORY BEGAN THE NEXT DAY. OVER 300 PLANES, MANY SHIPS, AND EVEN A FEW SUBMARINES TOOK PART.

HAITI

NOTHING WAS EVER FOUND.

PUERTO RICO

WHAT HAPPENED TO ALL THOSE MISSING PLANES AND SHIPS?

I'M A RAY FISH!

IT'S STILL A MYSTERY!

I'M GOING TO BE A MOVIE STAR.

THE LOCH NESS MONSTER

In 1933, a Scottish couple was driving along a new, modern road on the northern shore of Loch Ness. (*Loch* is the Scottish word for "lake.") Suddenly, their attention was drawn to the center of the lake. They later claimed that what they saw there was an enormous animal "rolling and plunging" in the water. Since that day, there have been more than 3,000 reported sightings of the Loch Ness monster.

LEARN ABOUT THE LOCH NESS MONSTER AS YOU LOOK FOR THESE FUN ITEMS:

- ❑ Astronaut
- ❑ Balloons (4)
- ❑ Bone
- ❑ Bucket
- ❑ Cameras (2)
- ❑ Clown
- ❑ Duck

- ❑ Fishbowl
- ❑ Flower
- ❑ Ghost
- ❑ Golfer
- ❑ Lost boot
- ❑ Mouse

- ❑ Mummy
- ❑ Net
- ❑ Note in a bottle
- ❑ Periscope
- ❑ Pig
- ❑ Sailboat

- ❑ Shorts
- ❑ Skateboard
- ❑ Star
- ❑ Sword
- ❑ Telescope

- ❑ Top hat
- ❑ Turtle

What is the monster's nickname?
How deep is Loch Ness?

STONEHENGE

Stonehenge is an ancient monument built on Salisbury Plain in Wiltshire, England. For centuries, scientists have puzzled over the circular arrangement of this group of huge, rough-cut stones and holes in the ground. Archaeologists believe that Stonehenge was shaped and positioned by a group of people more than 3,000 years ago, without the aid of modern tools and equipment. No one knows exactly how this was accomplished.

THIS MUST BE THE PLACE.

STONEHENGE IS A STRANGE CIRCULAR ARRANGEMENT OF STONES AND HOLES IN THE GROUND.

ACCORDING TO AN EARLY LEGEND, THE GREAT STONE CIRCLE WAS WHISKED TO THIS SPOT ONE NIGHT BY MERLIN!

I DON'T REMEMBER DOING THAT!!

SOME BELIEVE IT WAS A RELIGIOUS TEMPLE BUILT BY THE LEADERS OF ANCIENT BRITON — THE DRUIDS.

STONES WEIGHING UP TO ONE HUNDRED THOUSAND POUNDS EACH.

ARCHAEOLOGISTS BELIEVE STONEHENGE WAS BUILT IN THREE STAGES BY PEOPLE OTHER THAN THE DRUIDS!

CARVINGS ON THE STONES SHOW THE STONES ARE OVER 3,300 YEARS OLD.

MANY PEOPLE WORKED ON STONEHENGE OVER THE CENTURIES.

STONEHENGE IS LAID OUT AS A SERIES OF CIRCLES INSIDE EACH OTHER.

OINK.

THE OUTERMOST CIRCLE IS A LARGE DITCH.

INSIDE THIS IS AN EARTH WALL ABOUT 320 FEET IN DIAMETER.

TOWARD THE CENTER ARE LARGE SANDSTONE BLOCKS.

A CONTINUOUS CIRCLE OF SMALLER BLOCKS, CALLED LINTEL STONES, ARE ON TOP OF THEM.

INSIDE IS A CIRCLE OF 30 SMALLER BLUESTONES.

INSIDE THIS CIRCLE ARE TWO HORSE-SHOE-SHAPED SETS OF STONE — ONE OF SANDSTONE, THE OTHER OF BLUESTONE — ONE INSIDE THE OTHER. THESE OPENED TOWARD THE NORTHEAST.

NEXT COMES A CIRCLE OF EVENLY SPACED HOLES IN THE GROUND.

10

- ❏ Arrow
- ❏ Bird
- ❏ Bone
- ❏ Book
- ❏ Clown face
- ❏ Cooking pot
- ❏ Crown
- ❏ Cupcake
- ❏ Duck
- ❏ Elephant
- ❏ Flower
- ❏ Flying saucer
- ❏ Football
- ❏ Guitar
- ❏ Handbag
- ❏ Horse
- ❏ Jogger
- ❏ Magic wand
- ❏ Merlin
- ❏ Palm tree
- ❏ Pencil
- ❏ Pickaxe
- ❏ Pig
- ❏ Rabbit
- ❏ Shovel
- ❏ Teapot
- ❏ Tennis racket
- ❏ Turtle
- ❏ Umbrella
- ❏ Worm

How many stones were used to build Stonehenge? How much do the heaviest stones weigh?

AMELIA EARHART

In the early 20th century, flight was a new and sometimes frightening wonder. In 1908, when Amelia Earhart first saw an airplane soar among the clouds, she was fascinated by flight. Earhart became a pioneer in the new world of aviation. In 1932, she became the first woman to fly solo across the Atlantic Ocean.

LEARN ABOUT AMELIA EARHART AS YOU LOOK FOR THESE FUN ITEMS:

- ❑ Apple
- ❑ Basketball hoop
- ❑ Bell
- ❑ Chef's hat
- ❑ Envelope
- ❑ File folder
- ❑ Fish (2)
- ❑ Fishbowl
- ❑ Football
- ❑ Fork
- ❑ Graduate
- ❑ Hamburger
- ❑ Hammer
- ❑ Jack-o'-lantern
- ❑ Key
- ❑ Lost sock
- ❑ Magnifying glass
- ❑ Mouse
- ❑ Nurse
- ❑ Old-fashioned radio
- ❑ Old-fashioned telephone
- ❑ Paper airplane
- ❑ Pencil
- ❑ Pizza
- ❑ Seal
- ❑ Target
- ❑ Tennis racket
- ❑ Toaster
- ❑ TV set
- ❑ Typewriter
- ❑ Wastepaper basket
- ❑ Yo-yo

What was Amelia Earhart's great ambition as a pilot?

AFTER THE WAR SHE ATTENDED COLUMBIA UNIVERSITY.

HER REAL LOVE WAS FLYING. SHE DROPPED OUT TO EARN MONEY FOR FLYING LESSONS.

SHE LEARNED TO FLY IN LOS ANGELES, CALIFORNIA AND IN 1928 BECAME THE FIRST WOMAN TO FLY ACROSS THE ATLANTIC OCEAN.

SHE FLEW WITH WILBUR STUNTZ AND LOUIS GORDON.

THE PLANE WAS NAMED "FRIENDSHIP!"

SHE WROTE A BOOK ABOUT HER FLIGHT AND LATER MARRIED HER PUBLISHER, GEORGE PUTNAM.

THEY FLEW IN A TWIN-ENGINE LOCKHEED 10-E ELECTRA AIRPLANE.

THE PLANE VANISHED SOMEWHERE BETWEEN NEW GUINEA AND HOWLAND ISLAND.

SOME THINK THAT THEY WERE SHOT DOWN BY THE JAPANESE WHO BELIEVED THEY WERE ON A SECRET SPY MISSION.

OTHERS BELIEVE HER PLANE RAN OUT OF FUEL AND WENT DOWN IN THE OCEAN.

THESE ARE GREAT COMIC STRIPS FOR OUR SCHOOL PAPER.

FREDDIE, LISA, AND LAURA ARE IN IT.

AMELIA EARHART'S FIRST ATTEMPT AT A ROUND-THE-WORLD FLIGHT ALMOST ENDED IN TRAGEDY. A TIRE BLOW-OUT WHILE TAXIING RESULTED IN CONSIDERABLE DAMAGE TO THE PLANE....

WHEN HER LOCKHEED ELECTRA WAS REPAIRED, MISS EARHART CHANGED HER DIRECTION. WITH NAVIGATOR FRED NOONAN, SHE TOOK OFF IN HER "FLYING LABORATORY," HEADING EASTWARD OUT OF MIAMI, ON THE GRAY MORNING OF JUNE 1, 1937.

WHEN AMELIA EARHART TOOK OFF ON HER ROUND-THE-WORLD FLIGHT, HER PLANE WAS WELL-EQUIPPED WITH RUBBER RAFTS, FLARES, AND OTHER SAFETY DEVICES. ENOUGH SURVIVAL EQUIPMENT TO MEET ALMOST ANY EVENTUALITY....

MISS EARHART FLEW A SOUTH EASTERLY ROUTE FROM MIAMI TO SOUTH AMERICA; THEN ON TO AFRICA. FROM THERE, SHE EASILY HOPPED TO INDIA AND ACROSS TO BATAVIA....

MIAMI
AFRICA
INDIA
SOUTH AMERICA
BATAVIA

HOWLAND ISLAND WAS TO BE THE LAST STOP BEFORE HONOLULU. A TINY, 2-MILE-SQUARE SPECK IN THE OCEAN....A DIFFICULT TARGET FOR ANY PILOT....

AT 7:42 A.M., ON JULY 2, 1937, THE U.S. CUTTER ITASCA, WAITING AT HOWLAND ISLAND, RECEIVED THIS RADIO MESSAGE: "WE MUST BE ON YOU, BUT WE CANNOT SEE YOU. GAS IS RUNNING LOW. BEEN UNABLE TO REACH YOU BY RADIO...."

DURING THE NEXT DAYS, ONE OF THE LARGEST SEARCHES IN HISTORY TOOK PLACE. MEN, SHIPS, AND PLANES OF THREE NATIONS, INCLUDING JAPANESE AIRCRAFT, ENGAGED IN THE TREMENDOUS, EXHAUSTIVE HUNT....

2-J-14

THE OPERATION COST $1,000,000! THAT WAS 55 YEARS AGO. NOT ONE AUTHENTICATED CLUE TO THE FATE OF MISS EARHART, NAVIGATOR NOONAN, OR THEIR PLANE HAS EVER BEEN FOUND!

107

13

KING TUT'S CURSE

Howard Carter's 30-year search was over. On November 26, 1922, he stood before the entrance to the lost tomb of "the boy king," Tutankhamen *(too-tang-KAHM-un)*. Entering, Carter stared in disbelief at the gold, jewels, and other treasures before him. However, that day, a hawk—sacred symbol of pharaohs, the kings of ancient Egypt—was seen soaring above the tomb. Many people say that the hawk signalled the beginning of the pharaoh's curse.

LEARN ABOUT KING TUT'S CURSE AS YOU LOOK FOR THESE FUN ITEMS:

- ❑ Balloon
- ❑ Banana peel
- ❑ Broom
- ❑ Camel
- ❑ Crown
- ❑ Fish
- ❑ Flying bat
- ❑ Football player
- ❑ Ghost
- ❑ Horn
- ❑ Horseshoe
- ❑ Kite
- ❑ Lost medal
- ❑ Mouse
- ❑ Mummy and child
- ❑ Pencil
- ❑ Pizza deliveryman
- ❑ Sailor
- ❑ Sand
- ❑ Shovel
- ❑ Skier
- ❑ Snake
- ❑ Snowman
- ❑ Star
- ❑ Top hat
- ❑ Vase

What happened to Lord Carnarvon?
What was unusual about the scar on Tut's cheek?

15

ATLANTIS

The idea of a perfect world—one filled with beauty, peace, and happiness—had kept people searching for the lost island of Atlantis for centuries. Was Atlantis a real place, or just a myth of ancient Egypt made popular by Plato?

LEARN ABOUT ATLANTIS AS YOU LOOK FOR THESE FUN ITEMS:

- ☐ Ant
- ☐ Axe
- ☐ Book
- ☐ Chef's hat
- ☐ Chicken
- ☐ Deep-sea diver
- ☐ Deer
- ☐ Elephant
- ☐ Flamingo
- ☐ Frog
- ☐ Guitar
- ☐ Heart
- ☐ Ice-cream cone
- ☐ Kite
- ☐ Lion
- ☐ Mermaid
- ☐ Owl
- ☐ Ox
- ☐ Paintbrush
- ☐ Pelican
- ☐ Periscope
- ☐ Pig
- ☐ Rhinoceros
- ☐ Snail
- ☐ Snake
- ☐ Sock
- ☐ Toucan
- ☐ Turtle
- ☐ Umbrella
- ☐ Unicorn
- ☐ Zebra

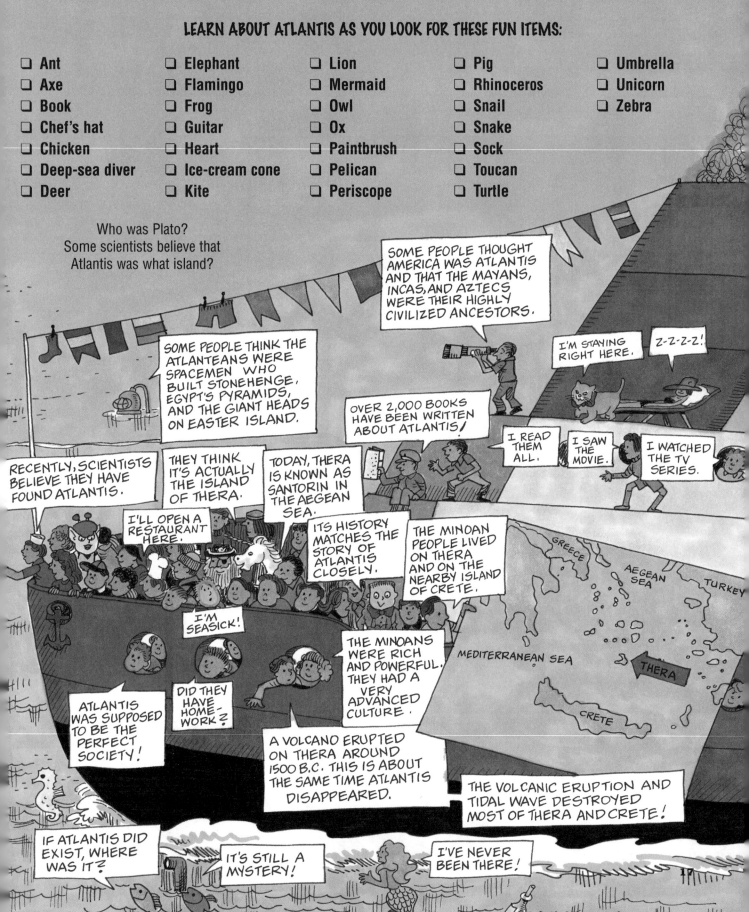

THE TUNGUSKA EXPLOSION

On June 30, 1908, the sky over the icy wilderness of Siberia flashed with a bright streak of light. Suddenly, the earth shook and smoke and fire shot up into the sky, reaching a height of 10 miles. This explosion was so tremendous, it was recorded around the world.

LEARN ABOUT THE TUNGUSKA EXPLOSION AS YOU LOOK FOR THESE FUN ITEMS:

- ❑ Arrow
- ❑ Bear
- ❑ Bell
- ❑ Boot
- ❑ Camel
- ❑ Crayon
- ❑ Crown
- ❑ Cupcake
- ❑ Doll
- ❑ Drum
- ❑ Elephant
- ❑ Fish
- ❑ Flashlight
- ❑ Flying bat
- ❑ Football
- ❑ Fork
- ❑ Ghost
- ❑ Heart
- ❑ Hot-air balloon
- ❑ Hot dog
- ❑ Igloo
- ❑ Jack-o'-lantern
- ❑ Key
- ❑ Kite
- ❑ Lips
- ❑ Mailbox
- ❑ Mask
- ❑ Mouse
- ❑ Pillow
- ❑ Ring
- ❑ Sailboat
- ❑ Skis
- ❑ Snake
- ❑ Tin can
- ❑ Tire
- ❑ Toothbrush
- ❑ Top hat
- ❑ Tree
- ❑ Tulip
- ❑ Turtle

What is a meteorite? When were atomic bombs first produced?

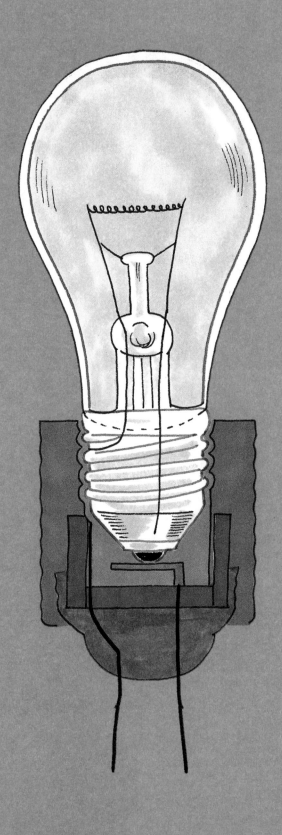

HOW THINGS WORK

COMPUTERS

Rare just a generation ago, computers are now everywhere! As technological know-how improves, these devices keep getting smaller, faster, more reliable, and easier to use.

LEARN ABOUT COMPUTERS AS YOU LOOK FOR THESE FUN ITEMS:

- ☐ Bears (2)
- ☐ Birds (2)
- ☐ Fish (3)
- ☐ Flowers (2)
- ☐ Ghosts (3)
- ☐ Horses (2)
- ☐ Neckerchief
- ☐ Pencils (2)
- ☐ Scarves (2)
- ☐ Sheet of paper
- ☐ Snail
- ☐ Snake
- ☐ Sunglasses (2)
- ☐ Volcanoes (2)

What is another word for modulator/demodulator?
What do *RAM* and *ROM* stand for?

DATA USED BY COMPUTERS ARE STORED ON VARIOUS TYPES OF DEVICES KNOWN AS DISKS. EACH COMPUTER HAS A HARD DISK, WHERE PROGRAMS, FILES, DOCUMENTS, AND OTHER KEY INFORMATION ARE STORED.

DATA STORED ON A COMPUTER'S HARD DRIVE CAN BE COPIED TO REMOVABLE DISKS AND STORED ELSEWHERE. FLOPPY DISKS, CDS, ZIP DISKS, AND DVDs ARE WIDELY USED STORAGE MEDIA.

A MICROCHIP IS A TINY BUT POWERFUL DEVICE THAT CAN HOLD AN IMMENSE AMOUNT OF DATA. AS MICROCHIPS HAVE GOTTEN SMALLER WHILE HOLDING MORE DATA, COMPUTERS HAVE BECOME SMALLER, TOO.

HARDWARE THAT YOU CAN SEE INCLUDES THE SYSTEM UNIT (CPU), MONITOR, KEYBOARD, MOUSE, AND STORAGE DEVICES (SUCH AS FLOPPY DISK, CD-ROM, OR DVD DRIVES).

A PERSONAL COMPUTER (PC) IS ONE THAT IS MEANT TO BE USED BY ONLY ONE PERSON AT A TIME. MOST PEOPLE USE THE WORD *PC* TO DESCRIBE A DESKTOP COMPUTER, BUT LAPTOP AND HAND-HELD COMPUTERS ARE ALSO ONE-PERSON-AT-A-TIME DEVICES.

HARDWARE THAT YOU CAN'T SEE—BECAUSE IT'S INSIDE THE SYSTEM UNIT—INCLUDES THE PROCESSOR AND MEMORY CHIPS.

A KEYBOARD IS USED LIKE A TYPEWRITER. WHEN YOU PRESS A KEY, INFORMATION APPEARS ON THE SCREEN.

THE SCANNER IS LIKE A CAMERA AND COPY MACHINE ROLLED INTO ONE DEVICE. USING LIGHT, MIRRORS, AND LENSES, IT TURNS AN IMAGE INTO DATA THAT YOUR COMPUTER CAN USE.

DO THEY STILL USE PENCILS?

PROGRAMS FOR WORD PROCESSING, WEB BROWSING, E-MAIL, PLAYING GAMES, AND MAKING SPREAD-SHEETS OR DATABASES ARE ALL EXAMPLES OF SOFTWARE.

FOR A COMPUTER TO WORK, YOU NEED BOTH HARDWARE AND SOFTWARE. HARDWARE IS THE EQUIPMENT THAT DOES THE WORK. SOFTWARE IS INFORMATION THAT TELLS THE EQUIPMENT WHAT TO DO AND HOW TO DO IT.

YOUR COMPUTER MAY HAVE OTHER HARDWARE CALLED *PERIPHERALS*—DEVICES INSTALLED IN OR ATTACHED TO YOUR COMPUTER TO EXPAND WHAT IT CAN DO. COMMON PERIPHERALS INCLUDE MODEMS, PRINTERS, AND SCANNERS.

THE MODEM IS A DEVICE THAT LETS TWO OR MORE COMPUTERS "TALK" TO EACH OTHER. MODEMS SEND SIGNALS THROUGH TELEPHONE, CABLE, OR OTHER COMMUNICATIONS LINES. (MODEM IS SHORT FOR "MOdulator/ DEModulator.")

LIGHT BULBS

An electric light bulb is a glass bulb that contains a filament, an inert gas, and electrical contacts. Light is produced when an electrical current passes through the filament. This current heats the filament to a temperature that is high enough to produce light.

Thomas Edison invented the light bulb in 1879.

LEARN HOW LIGHT BULBS WORK AS YOU LOOK FOR THESE FUN ITEMS:

- ❏ Alarm clock
- ❏ Apple
- ❏ Baby's bib
- ❏ Baseball bat
- ❏ Bone
- ❏ Burned-out bulb
- ❏ Candles (2)
- ❏ Clipboard

- ❏ Clown
- ❏ Crayon
- ❏ Elephant
- ❏ Envelope
- ❏ Fish (2)
- ❏ Flowers (2)
- ❏ Football
- ❏ Fork

- ❏ Ghost
- ❏ Heart
- ❏ Helmet
- ❏ Horse's head
- ❏ Horseshoe
- ❏ Hose
- ❏ Jump rope
- ❏ Necktie

- ❏ Paintbrush
- ❏ Paper bag
- ❏ Pencil
- ❏ Pizza box
- ❏ Saw
- ❏ Tepee
- ❏ Used tire
- ❏ Vest

What is a filament made of?
What determines the brightness of a light bulb?

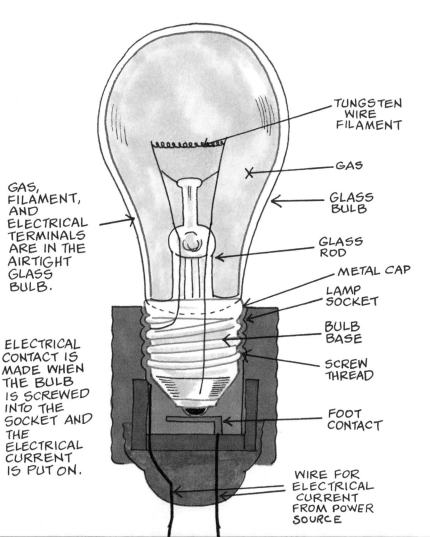

DON'T TURN THE LIGHT ON! I LIKE THE DARK!

YOU WON'T NEED ME.

GAS, FILAMENT, AND ELECTRICAL TERMINALS ARE IN THE AIRTIGHT GLASS BULB.

ELECTRICAL CONTACT IS MADE WHEN THE BULB IS SCREWED INTO THE SOCKET AND THE ELECTRICAL CURRENT IS PUT ON.

I WAS MADE THE SAME WAY!

TUNGSTEN WIRE FILAMENT

GAS

GLASS BULB

GLASS ROD

METAL CAP

LAMP SOCKET

BULB BASE

SCREW THREAD

FOOT CONTACT

WIRE FOR ELECTRICAL CURRENT FROM POWER SOURCE

IT'S DARK IN THIS ROOM! I'LL TURN THE LIGHT ON!

27

SUBMARINES

A submarine is designed to travel under water. Aided by small moveable fins called *hydroplanes*, it dives and surfaces by filling its ballast tanks with water or air. When the tanks are filled with water, the sub gets heavier and sinks. When compressed air is blown into the tanks, forcing out the water, the sub gets lighter and rises. Power to drive the sub comes from a nuclear reactor or from a combination of diesel and battery-driven engines.

LEARN HOW SUBS WORK AS YOU LOOK FOR THESE FUN ITEMS:

- ❏ Bathtub
- ❏ Book
- ❏ Cactus
- ❏ Clothespins (2)
- ❏ Crown
- ❏ Fish hook
- ❏ Four-leaf clover
- ❏ Frog
- ❏ Ghost
- ❏ Hammer
- ❏ Jellyfish
- ❏ Light bulb
- ❏ Mermaid
- ❏ Mouse
- ❏ Pizza
- ❏ Propellers (3)
- ❏ Sea horse
- ❏ Tuba

What was the *Turtle*? What do hydroplanes do?

28

HELICOPTERS

Helicopters can fly straight up or down, forward or backward, or sideways; and they can even hover in place. Their mobility allows them to fly into places that airplanes cannot.

The first helicopter to achieve flight was built in France in 1907. It was not reliable, however. In 1939, Igor Sikorsky developed the first successful one, and the modern era of helicopters began.

LEARN HOW HELICOPTERS WORK AS YOU LOOK FOR THESE FUN ITEMS:

- ❏ Balloon
- ❏ Bee
- ❏ Book
- ❏ Bucket
- ❏ Butterfly
- ❏ Cactus
- ❏ Camera
- ❏ Candy cane
- ❏ Canteen
- ❏ Flying bat
- ❏ Frog
- ❏ Heart
- ❏ Jack-o'-lantern
- ❏ Lollipop
- ❏ Medal
- ❏ Mouse
- ❏ Oilcan
- ❏ Owl
- ❏ Paper airplane
- ❏ Penguin
- ❏ Periscope
- ❏ Roller skates
- ❏ Schoolbag
- ❏ Screwdriver
- ❏ Squirrel
- ❏ Tennis racket

How many main rotor blades do most helicopters have?
What gives a helicopter its power?

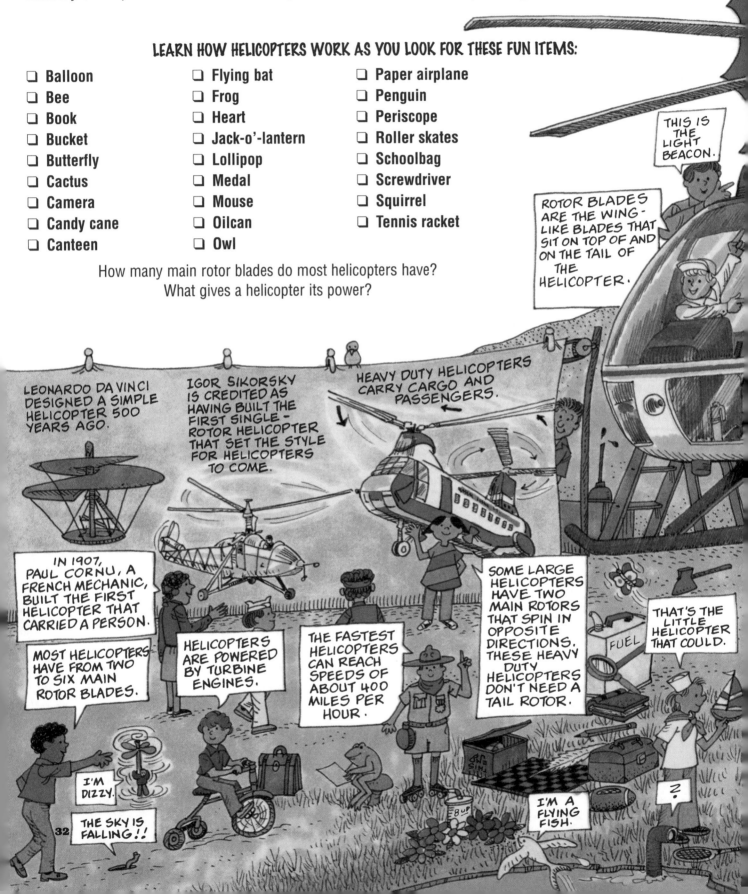

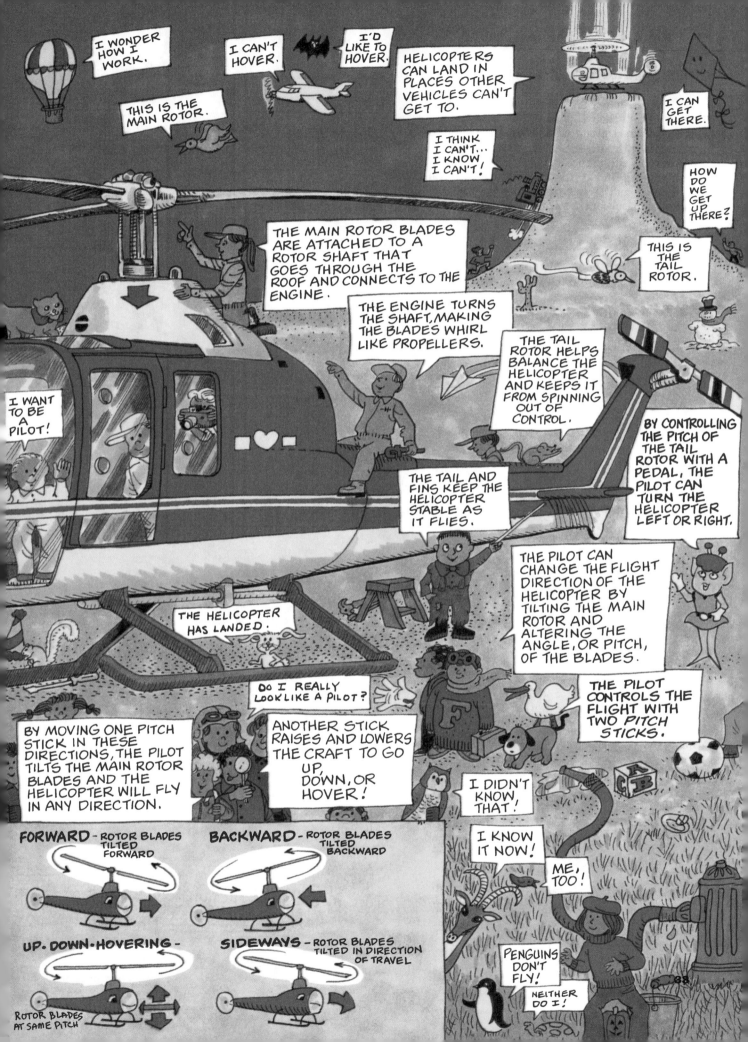

ORCHESTRAS

An orchestra is not a random gathering of musicians and their instruments. It is a carefully planned group of different types of instruments, with each one having its own part to play in the performance.

LEARN HOW ORCHESTRAS WORK AS YOU LOOK FOR THESE FUN ITEMS:

- ❑ **Ball of string**
- ❑ **Balloon**
- ❑ **Baseball cap**
- ❑ **Bird**
- ❑ **Broom**
- ❑ **Brush**
- ❑ **Candle**
- ❑ **Duck**
- ❑ **Earring**

VIBRAPHONE

TIMPANI

TUBA

FRENCH HORNS

CLARINETS

FLUTES

VIOLAS

PIANO

STRINGS SECTION

FIRST VIOLINS

OOPS! WRONG STAGE!

I'M THE MUSICAL SPIRIT.

WHO PUT SOAP IN MY SAXOPHONE?

I'M THE KITTEN ON THE PIANO STRINGS.

THE SYMPHONY ORCHESTRA IS THE LARGEST ORCHESTRA.

IT IS MADE UP OF ABOUT 90 MUSICIANS.

I PLAY THE RADIO.

THE PRINCIPAL VIOLINIST LEADS ALL THE OTHER MUSICIANS

THE SYMPHONY ORCHESTRA IS DIVIDED INTO FOUR MAIN SECTIONS OF INSTRUMENTS. THEY ARE: STRINGS, WOODWINDS, BRASS, AND PERCUSSION.

INSTRUMENTS IN THE STRING SECTION INCLUDE: FIRST AND SECOND VIOLINS, CELLO, VIOLA, DOUBLE BASS, HARP, AND PIANO.

INSTRUMENTS IN THE WOODWIND SECTION INCLUDE: FLUTE, PICCOLO, CLARINET, SAXOPHONE, OBOE, AND BASSOON.

INSTRUMENTS IN THE BRASS SECTION INCLUDE: TRUMPET, TUBA, FRENCH HORN, AND TROMBONE.

INSTRUMENTS IN THE PERCUSSION SECTION INCLUDE: DRUMS, GONG, VIBRAPHONE, AND TIMPANI.

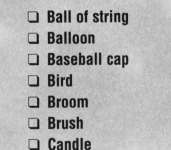

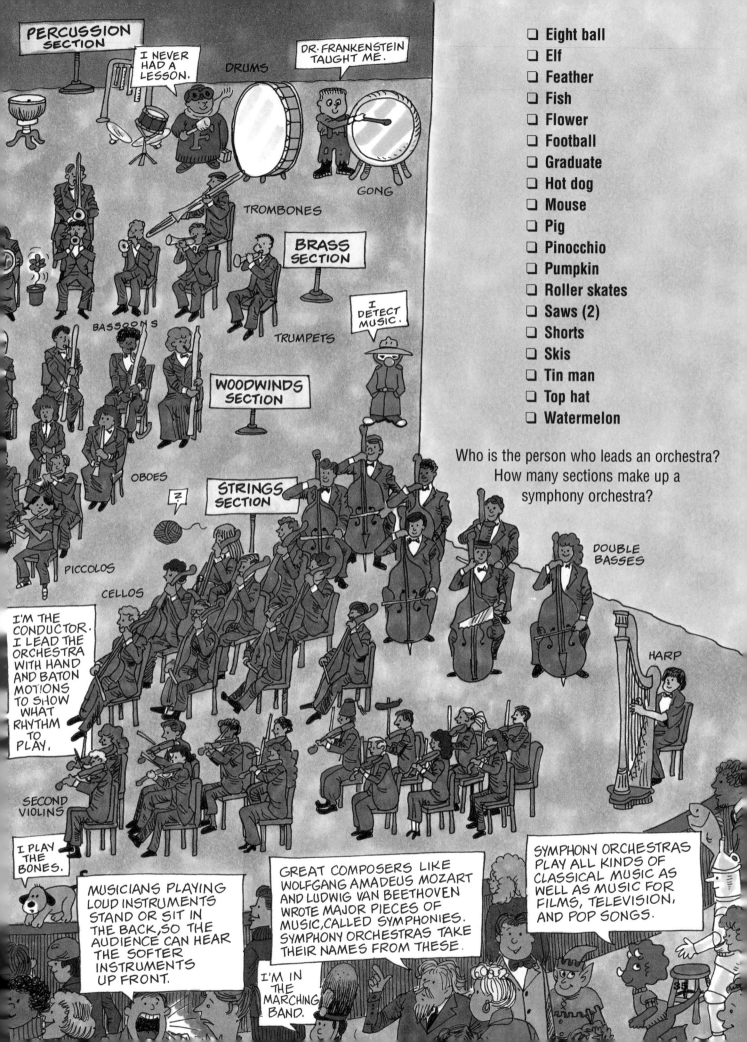

CDS AND DVDS

Whether it's music or movies that you love best, CDs and DVDs make it possible for you to take your favorite tunes and flicks almost anywhere. Those data-packed little plastic disks are a marvel of modern technology.

LEARN ABOUT CDs AND DVDs AS YOU LOOK FOR THESE FUN ITEMS:

- ❑ Apple
- ❑ Balloons (2)
- ❑ Banana peel
- ❑ Boat in a bottle
- ❑ Book
- ❑ Bowling ball
- ❑ Broom
- ❑ Butterfly
- ❑ Candle
- ❑ Clown
- ❑ Crown
- ❑ Donkey
- ❑ Flower
- ❑ Flying saucer
- ❑ Football
- ❑ Hairbrush
- ❑ Jack-o'-lantern
- ❑ Magnifying glass
- ❑ Paper airplane
- ❑ Picnic basket
- ❑ Scarves (2)
- ❑ Scissors
- ❑ Shovel
- ❑ Tent

DVDS ARE PRETTY MUCH THE SAME AS CDS, ONLY THEY'RE BUILT TO HOLD MORE DATA—ABOUT SEVEN TIMES MORE.

UNLIKE CDs, DVDs CAN HAVE 2 LAYERS OF BUMPS, NOT JUST ONE. THEY CAN BE 2-SIDED, AS WELL, WHICH ALLOWS THEM TO HOLD ALL THAT EXTRA DATA.

A DVD CAN HOLD UP TO 133 MINUTES OF HIGH-RESOLUTION VIDEO.

DVDS CAN PRESENT SOUNDTRACKS IN UP TO EIGHT LANGUAGES, AND SUBTITLES IN UP TO 32 LANGUAGES.

DVDS HAVE THE SAME PLASTIC AND ALUMINUM LAYERS AS CDS HAVE. DVDS, HOWEVER, ALSO HAVE A THIN GOLD LAYER.

THE GOLD LAYER ALLOWS THE LASER TO FOCUS THROUGH THE OUTER LAYERS TO THE INNER LAYERS OF THE DVD.

CDs AND DVDs ALSO STORE INFORMATION ABOUT ERROR CORRECTION, TO ENSURE THAT THEY'RE READ PROPERLY.

EVEN THOUGH DVDs HOLD LOTS OF DATA, A FULL-LENGTH MOVIE IS STILL TOO LONG FOR JUST ONE DVD.

TO FIT A MOVIE ON ONE DVD, THE MOVIE HAS TO BE ELECTRONICALLY COMPRESSED.

WHEN YOU POP A DVD INTO A PLAYER, THE PLAYER UNCOMPRESSES THE DATA AND PLAYS THE MOVIE.

WHERE'S THE POPCORN?

HE'S A DING-DONG!

NOW IF THEY COULD ONLY MAKE BETTER MOVIES!

WHERE'S THE PIZZA I ORDERED?

IF THE DATA TRACK ON A DVD WERE UNRAVELED, IT WOULD BE 7.5 MILES LONG.

THE DATA TRACK ON A DOUBLE-LAYERED, DOUBLE-SIDED DVD WOULD BE MORE THAN 30 MILES LONG.

POP! POP! POP! POP! POP! POP!

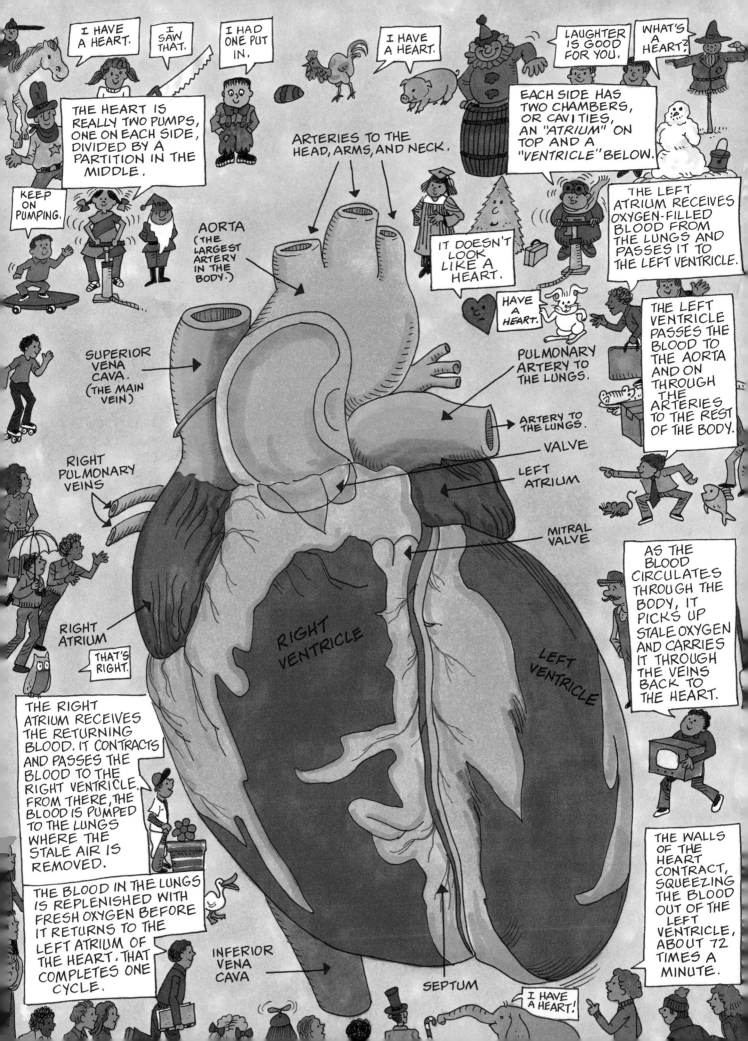

THE HUMAN HEART

A heart is a muscular pump that circulates blood through the blood vessels. The blood carries nourishment and oxygen to every part of the body. In one year, the human heart pumps about 650,000 gallons of blood, enough to fill 50 swimming pools!

LEARN HOW THE HUMAN HEART WORKS AS YOU LOOK FOR THESE FUN ITEMS:

- ❑ Ball
- ❑ Banana peel
- ❑ Barrel
- ❑ Baseball hat
- ❑ Book
- ❑ Candy cane
- ❑ Chicken
- ❑ Dracula
- ❑ Drum
- ❑ Duck
- ❑ Flower
- ❑ Joggers (2)
- ❑ Lion
- ❑ Microscope
- ❑ Mouse
- ❑ Mustache
- ❑ Owl
- ❑ Pillow
- ❑ Propeller
- ❑ Roller skates
- ❑ Saw
- ❑ Singer
- ❑ Skateboard
- ❑ Stars (2)
- ❑ Top hat
- ❑ TV set
- ❑ Umbrella
- ❑ Worm

What are the heart's chambers called?

Approximately how long does it take for the blood to travel throughout the body?

SOLAR ENERGY

Solar energy is power produced by the sun. It can be used to heat and purify water, give power to engines, and produce electricity. A person would have to burn 550 billion tons of coal in order to equal the amount of solar energy received by Earth in one day!

LEARN HOW SOLAR ENERGY WORKS AS YOU LOOK FOR THESE FUN ITEMS:

- ❏ Apple
- ❏ Arrow
- ❏ Baseball
- ❏ Basketball hoop
- ❏ Bone
- ❏ Bowling ball
- ❏ Brush
- ❏ Buckets (2)
- ❏ Doghouse
- ❏ Duck
- ❏ Earmuffs
- ❏ Fire hydrant
- ❏ Flower
- ❏ Football
- ❏ Hammer
- ❏ Heart
- ❏ Helmet
- ❏ Kite
- ❏ Mailbox
- ❏ Newspaper
- ❏ Rabbit
- ❏ Screwdriver
- ❏ Star
- ❏ Turtle
- ❏ Umbrella
- ❏ Umpire
- ❏ Watering can
- ❏ Worm

What is solar power most commonly used for?
Why are the insides of solar panels painted black?

AIRPLANES

Airplanes are fascinating pieces of machinery that soar through the air. Whether passenger, private, or military, they all operate under the same aerodynamic principles.

The first power-driven flight was made by the Wright brothers at Kitty Hawk, North Carolina, in 1903.

LEARN HOW AIRPLANES WORK AS YOU LOOK FOR THESE FUN ITEMS:

- ❑ "X-1"
- ❑ Acrobat
- ❑ Banana
- ❑ Bowling ball
- ❑ Broom
- ❑ Elephant
- ❑ Fishing pole
- ❑ Flowers (3)
- ❑ Flying carpet
- ❑ Flying horse
- ❑ Flying saucer
- ❑ Football
- ❑ Ghost
- ❑ Glider
- ❑ Hamburger
- ❑ Hang glider
- ❑ Kite
- ❑ Mouse
- ❑ Paper airplane
- ❑ Pencil
- ❑ Pinwheel
- ❑ Pizza
- ❑ Sailboat
- ❑ Seaplane
- ❑ Sled
- ❑ Stars (2)
- ❑ Superheroes (2)
- ❑ Surfboard
- ❑ Umbrella
- ❑ Yo-yo

What provides an airplane's lift?
What kind of engine "pulls" the airplane through the air?

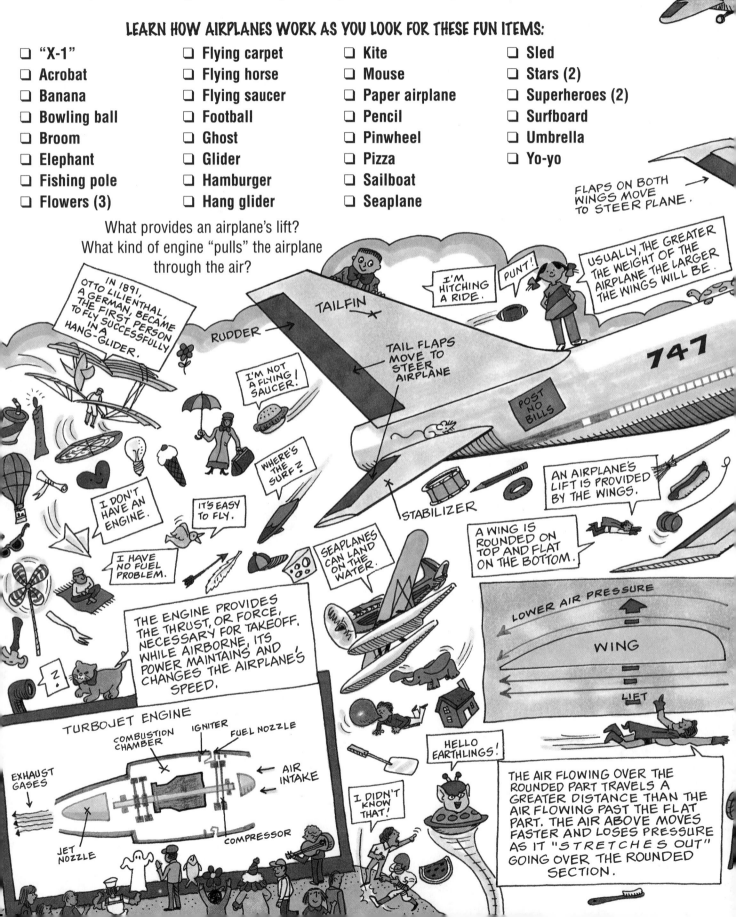

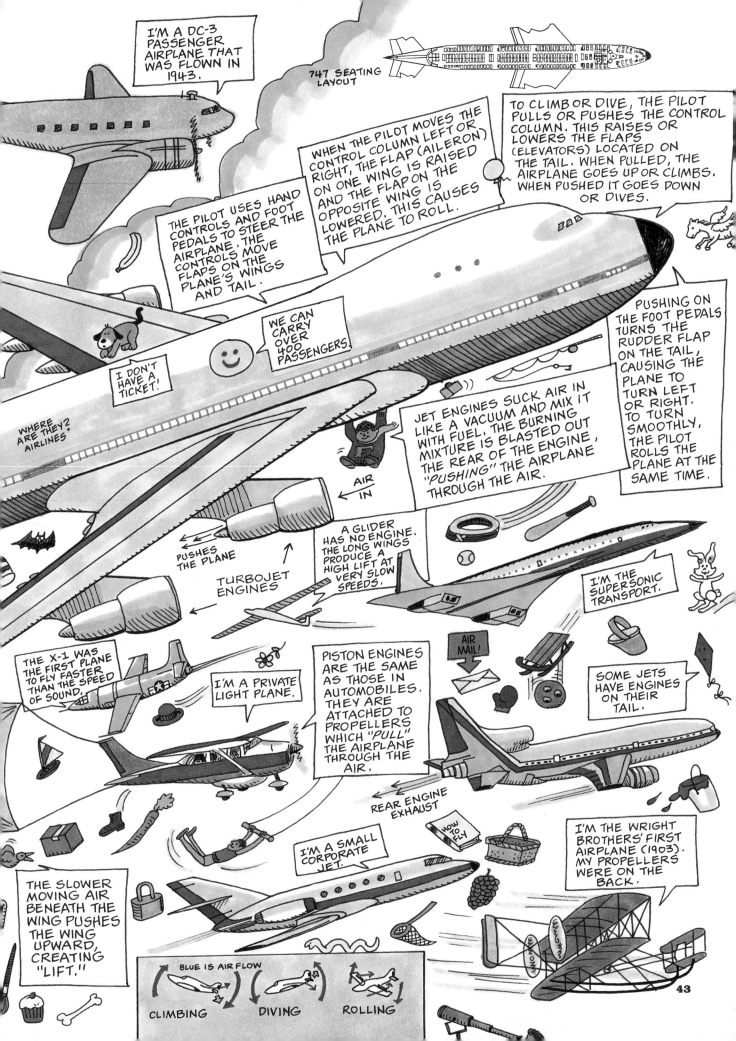

LASERS

A laser is a device that intensifies or increases light. It produces a thin beam of light, stronger than sunlight, that can burn a hole through diamond or steel.

The first operational laser was built in 1960.

LEARN HOW LASERS WORK AS YOU LOOK FOR THESE FUN ITEMS:

- ☐ Apple
- ☐ Book
- ☐ Cheerleader
- ☐ Chicken
- ☐ Clock
- ☐ Drinking straw
- ☐ Drum
- ☐ Electrodes (2)
- ☐ Envelope
- ☐ FIsh tank
- ☐ Flamingo
- ☐ Football
- ☐ Frog
- ☐ Globe
- ☐ Hot dog
- ☐ Little Red Riding Hood
- ☐ Necktie
- ☐ Orangutan
- ☐ Painted egg
- ☐ Paper airplane
- ☐ Parrot
- ☐ Rabbit
- ☐ Roller skates
- ☐ Stapler
- ☐ Stethoscope
- ☐ Thermometer
- ☐ Umbrella
- ☐ Vase

Name two types of lasers.
What are some of the uses of laser beams?

IN ORDINARY LIGHT, SUCH AS THAT FROM A LIGHT BULB, THE LIGHT WAVES GO OUT IN MANY DIFFERENT DIRECTIONS.

IN A LASER BEAM, THE LIGHT WAVES ALL HAVE THE SAME LENGTH AND TRAVEL IN THE SAME DIRECTION, PRODUCING A NARROW, INTENSE BEAM OF LIGHT.

HOORAY FOR LASERS!

IS THIS THE GYM CLASS?

I'M IN THE MARCHING BAND.

I DON'T NEED A GAS MASK.

IS IT TIME FOR LUNCH?

I WANT ONE.

LASERS COME IN MANY SHAPES AND SIZES.

SOLID-STATE LASERS USE A MATERIAL SUCH AS RUBY, EMERALD, OR GLASS CRYSTAL TO PRODUCE BURSTS OF LIGHT.

GAS LASERS ARE MADE IN A GAS-FILLED TUBE AND PRODUCE A CONTINUOUS BEAM OF LIGHT.

GAS LASER

GAS-FILLED TUBE

ELECTRODE

MIRROR

ELECTRODE

SEMI-SILVERED MIRROR

I'LL PUNCH YOU IN THE NOSE!

I DON'T HAVE A NOSE!

ONCE THE LIGHT IS BRIGHT ENOUGH, IT PASSES THROUGH A SEMI-SILVERED MIRROR AND LEAVES THE LASER.

THE MATERIAL USED TO CREATE LASER LIGHT IS CALLED A "MEDIUM." IT MAY BE SOLID, GAS, OR EVEN LIQUID.

TO PRODUCE A BEAM OF LASER LIGHT, ENERGY FROM A POWER SOURCE, SUCH AS AN ELECTRIC CURRENT, EXCITES THE ATOMS OF THE MEDIUM CAUSING THEM TO STRIKE EACH OTHER AND GIVE OFF LIGHT.

MIRRORS ARE USED WITHIN THE LASER TUBE TO INCREASE THE LIGHT-PRODUCING ATOM.

MAGNETS AND MAGNETISM

A magnet is often thought of as a toy that can pull or pick up metal objects. However, the invisible force of magnetism is used in a wide variety of modern devices.

Magnetite, an iron ore with magnetic properties, was used as a compass by early sailors to navigate.

LEARN HOW MAGNETS AND MAGNETISM WORK AS YOU LOOK FOR THESE FUN ITEMS:

- ❑ Bent nail
- ❑ Cactus
- ❑ Clown
- ❑ Compasses (2)
- ❑ Dart
- ❑ Duck
- ❑ Flower
- ❑ Football player
- ❑ Hard hats (2)
- ❑ Hooks (2)
- ❑ Hot dog
- ❑ Ice-cream cone
- ❑ Kangaroo
- ❑ Key
- ❑ Lion
- ❑ Mermaid
- ❑ Mouse
- ❑ Periscope
- ❑ Pillow
- ❑ Ringmaster
- ❑ Rocking chair
- ❑ Safety pin
- ❑ Sewing needle
- ❑ Shovel
- ❑ Snake
- ❑ Spoon
- ❑ Tin Man
- ❑ TV antenna

When is a metal magnetized?
Where are Earth's two magnetic poles?

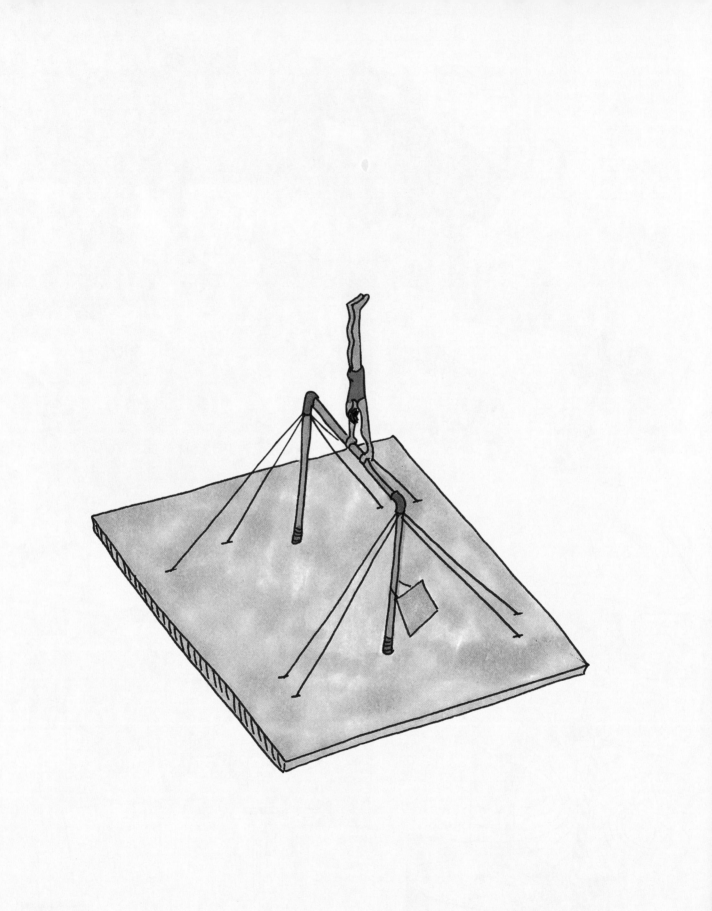

Sports

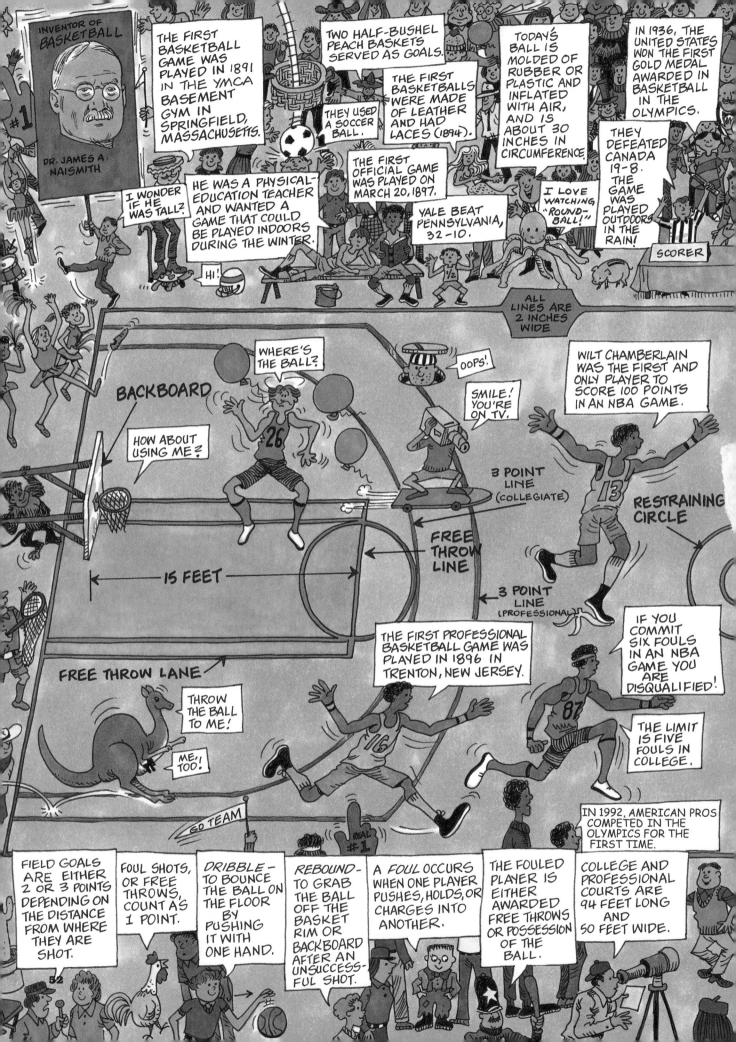

BASKETBALL

Basketball is played in more than 200 countries around the world. To play, all you need are a ball, a basket or hoop, and a level surface. Basketball can be played indoors or out, alone or with others, at night or by day, 365 days a year!

LEARN ABOUT BASKETBALL AS YOU LOOK FOR THESE FUN ITEMS:

- ❑ Balloons (5)
- ❑ Banana peel
- ❑ Bowling ball
- ❑ Boxing glove
- ❑ Bucket
- ❑ Cane
- ❑ Clock
- ❑ Crown
- ❑ Football
- ❑ Graduate
- ❑ Ice skate
- ❑ Kite
- ❑ Lost shoe
- ❑ Mermaid
- ❑ Monkey
- ❑ Mouse
- ❑ Pencil
- ❑ Piggy bank
- ❑ Scarecrow
- ❑ Skateboard
- ❑ Soccer ball
- ❑ Top hat
- ❑ Turtle

Name the NBA's career scoring leader.

GYMNASTICS

In gymnastics, acrobatic exercises are performed on various pieces of equipment. Gymnastics helps develop balance, agility, and strength. During the Olympics of 1972 and 1976, the emergence of two superstars—Olga Korbut and Nadia Comaneci—helped give gymnastics worldwide popularity.

LEARN ABOUT GYMNASTICS AS YOU LOOK FOR THESE FUN ITEMS:

- ❑ Banana peel
- ❑ Bear
- ❑ Broom
- ❑ Crutch
- ❑ Duck
- ❑ Elephant
- ❑ Juggler
- ❑ Kangaroo
- ❑ Mail carrier
- ❑ Pillow
- ❑ Scarecrow
- ❑ Snowman
- ❑ Star
- ❑ Telescope
- ❑ TV camera
- ❑ Unicorn
- ❑ Water skier

Who was the first Olympic gymnast to earn a perfect 10? Name the eight events in which men compete.

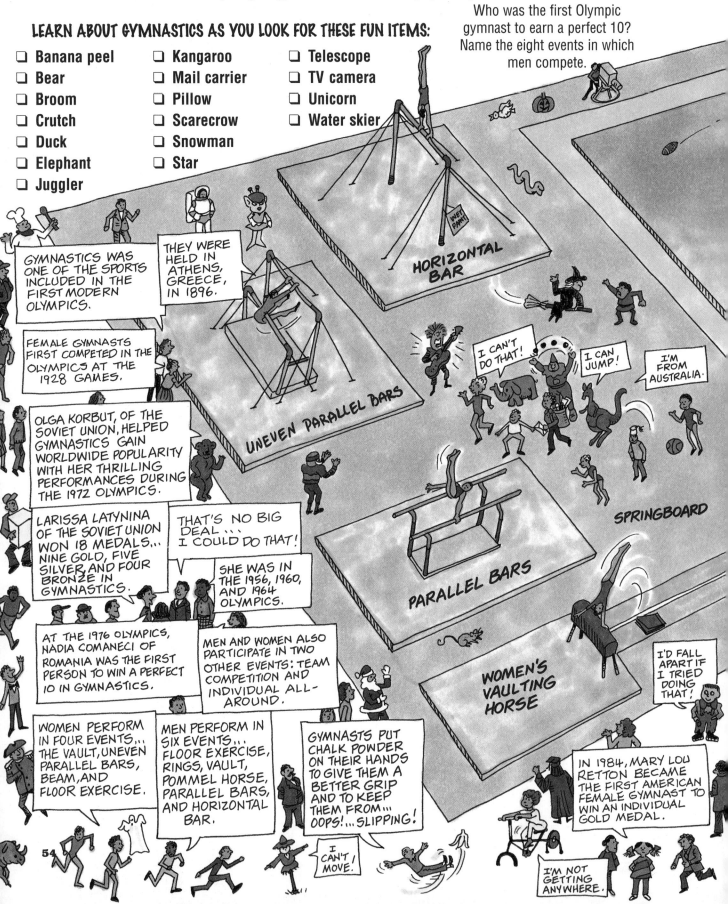

GYMNASTICS WAS ONE OF THE SPORTS INCLUDED IN THE FIRST MODERN OLYMPICS.

THEY WERE HELD IN ATHENS, GREECE, IN 1896.

HORIZONTAL BAR

WET PAINT

FEMALE GYMNASTS FIRST COMPETED IN THE OLYMPICS AT THE 1928 GAMES.

I CAN'T DO THAT!

I CAN JUMP!

I'M FROM AUSTRALIA.

OLGA KORBUT, OF THE SOVIET UNION, HELPED GYMNASTICS GAIN WORLDWIDE POPULARITY WITH HER THRILLING PERFORMANCES DURING THE 1972 OLYMPICS.

UNEVEN PARALLEL BARS

LARISSA LATYNINA OF THE SOVIET UNION WON 18 MEDALS,... NINE GOLD, FIVE SILVER, AND FOUR BRONZE IN GYMNASTICS.

THAT'S NO BIG DEAL... I COULD DO THAT!

SHE WAS IN THE 1956, 1960, AND 1964 OLYMPICS.

SPRINGBOARD

PARALLEL BARS

AT THE 1976 OLYMPICS, NADIA COMANECI OF ROMANIA WAS THE FIRST PERSON TO WIN A PERFECT 10 IN GYMNASTICS.

MEN AND WOMEN ALSO PARTICIPATE IN TWO OTHER EVENTS: TEAM COMPETITION AND INDIVIDUAL ALL-AROUND.

WOMEN'S VAULTING HORSE

I'D FALL APART IF I TRIED DOING THAT!

WOMEN PERFORM IN FOUR EVENTS,... THE VAULT, UNEVEN PARALLEL BARS, BEAM, AND FLOOR EXERCISE.

MEN PERFORM IN SIX EVENTS... FLOOR EXERCISE, RINGS, VAULT, POMMEL HORSE, PARALLEL BARS, AND HORIZONTAL BAR.

GYMNASTS PUT CHALK POWDER ON THEIR HANDS TO GIVE THEM A BETTER GRIP AND TO KEEP THEM FROM... OOPS!...SLIPPING!

IN 1984, MARY LOU RETTON BECAME THE FIRST AMERICAN FEMALE GYMNAST TO WIN AN INDIVIDUAL GOLD MEDAL.

I CAN'T MOVE!

I'M NOT GETTING ANYWHERE.

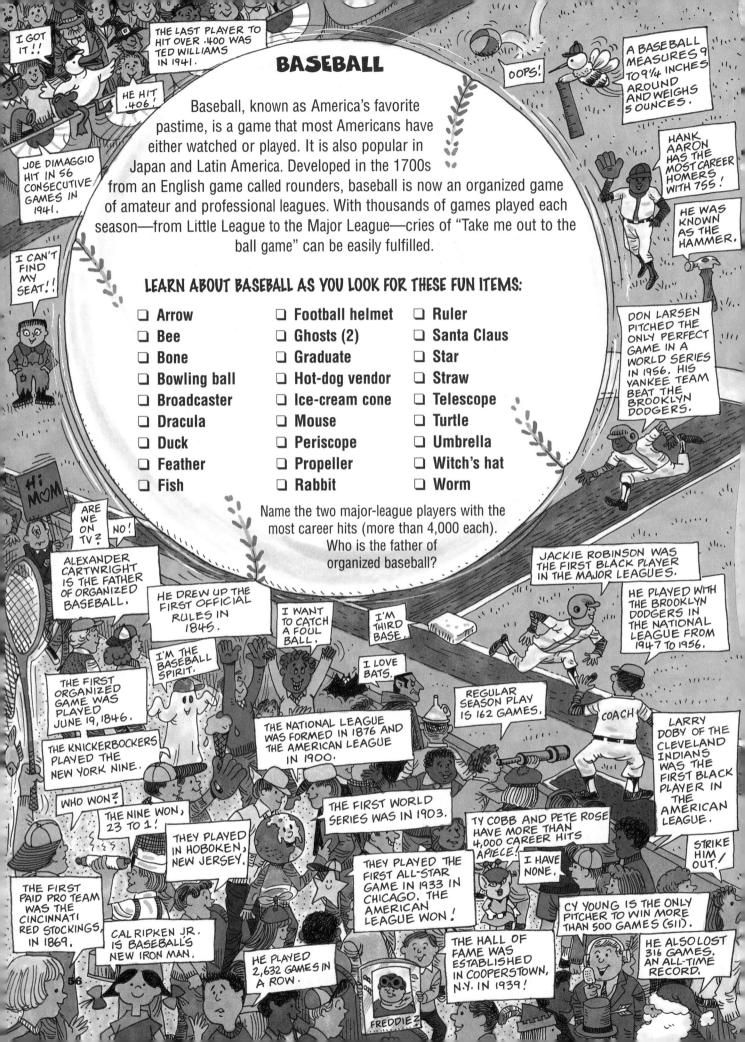

BASEBALL

Baseball, known as America's favorite pastime, is a game that most Americans have either watched or played. It is also popular in Japan and Latin America. Developed in the 1700s from an English game called rounders, baseball is now an organized game of amateur and professional leagues. With thousands of games played each season—from Little League to the Major League—cries of "Take me out to the ball game" can be easily fulfilled.

LEARN ABOUT BASEBALL AS YOU LOOK FOR THESE FUN ITEMS:

- ❏ Arrow
- ❏ Bee
- ❏ Bone
- ❏ Bowling ball
- ❏ Broadcaster
- ❏ Dracula
- ❏ Duck
- ❏ Feather
- ❏ Fish
- ❏ Football helmet
- ❏ Ghosts (2)
- ❏ Graduate
- ❏ Hot-dog vendor
- ❏ Ice-cream cone
- ❏ Mouse
- ❏ Periscope
- ❏ Propeller
- ❏ Rabbit
- ❏ Ruler
- ❏ Santa Claus
- ❏ Star
- ❏ Straw
- ❏ Telescope
- ❏ Turtle
- ❏ Umbrella
- ❏ Witch's hat
- ❏ Worm

Name the two major-league players with the most career hits (more than 4,000 each). Who is the father of organized baseball?

NASCAR RACING

NASCAR racing is fast becoming one of the most popular spectator sports in the U.S. With more than 7 million fans a year attending at NASCAR events, not all of the roars you'll hear at the track are coming from the car engines.

LEARN ABOUT NASCAR RACING AS YOU LOOK FOR THESE FUN ITEMS:

- ☐ Astronaut
- ☐ Balloon
- ☐ Birds (2)
- ☐ Bone
- ☐ Elephant
- ☐ Fish
- ☐ Flowers
- ☐ Heart
- ☐ Jockey
- ☐ Kangaroo
- ☐ Kite
- ☐ Pirate
- ☐ Rabbit
- ☐ Sailboat
- ☐ Scuba diver
- ☐ Oilcan
- ☐ Table
- ☐ Tepee
- ☐ Turtle

How long is the Daytona International Speedway?
Who won the first race there?

FOOTBALL

On November 6, 1869, the universities of Rutgers and Princeton met in New Brunswick, New Jersey, in the first college football game. Rutgers won it, 6–4.

The early games were a modified version of soccer and rugby. Football pioneers, such as Walter Camp, instituted 11-man teams, downs and yards to go, a smaller field, the line of scrimmage, and a new system of scoring.

LEARN ABOUT FOOTBALL AS YOU LOOK FOR THESE FUN ITEMS:

- ☐ Air pump
- ☐ Arrow
- ☐ Birds (3)
- ☐ Blimp
- ☐ Bowling pin
- ☐ Candy cane
- ☐ Clipboard
- ☐ Fish
- ☐ Flying bat
- ☐ Ghost
- ☐ Hamburger
- ☐ Heart
- ☐ Horseshoe
- ☐ Hot dog
- ☐ Locker
- ☐ Lost sneaker
- ☐ Mask
- ☐ Mummy
- ☐ Pencil
- ☐ Snowman
- ☐ Straw
- ☐ Telescope
- ☐ Trophy
- ☐ Turtle
- ☐ Water bucket
- ☐ Whistle
- ☐ Worm

What is a punt?
What is a player's shirt called?

OFFENSE:
C – CENTER
G – GUARD
WR – WIDE RECEIVER
T – TACKLE
TE – TIGHT END
QB – QUARTERBACK
B – BACK
DEFENSE:
DT – DEFENSIVE TACKLE
DE – DEFENSIVE END
LB – LINEBACKER
DB – DEFENSIVE BACK
FS – FREE SAFETY
SS – STRONG SAFETY
NT – NOSE TACKLE

THE FIRST PRO GAME WAS PLAYED IN LATROBE, PA.

THE NFL (NATIONAL FOOTBALL LEAGUE) WAS FORMED IN 1922.

THERE ARE 32 TEAMS IN THE NFL. THE CHAMPIONSHIP IS CALLED THE SUPER BOWL.

THE FIRST SUPER BOWL WAS PLAYED IN 1967. THE GREEN BAY PACKERS BEAT THE KANSAS CITY CHIEFS, 35-10.

THE FIELD IS 100 YARDS LONG AND 160 FEET WIDE.
THE FIELD IS ALSO CALLED THE GRIDIRON.

WHITE LINES, CALLED YARDLINES, RUN ACROSS THE FIELD EVERY FIVE YARDS.

TWO ROWS OF SHORT WHITE LINES, CALLED HASH MARKS, SET ONE YARD APART, ALSO RUN THE LENGTH OF FIELD. ALL PLAYS BEGIN WITH THE BALL ON OR BETWEEN THE HASH MARKS.

GOAL POST

END ZONE

50 YD. LINE

HURRY UP WITH THAT BALL!

THE AIR-FILLED LEATHER BALL WEIGHS 14-15 OUNCES AND IS ABOUT 11 INCHES FROM POINT TO POINT.

THE LACES PROVIDE A GOOD GRIP FOR PASSERS AND BALL CARRIERS.

CARRYING OR PASSING THE BALL INTO THE OPPONENT'S END ZONE IS A TOUCHDOWN... GOOD FOR 6 POINTS. AN EXTRA POINT CAN THEN BE MADE BY KICKING THE BALL THROUGH THE GOAL POSTS.

OTHER POINTS: FIELD GOAL – 3 POINTS. OCCURS WHEN THE BALL IS KICKED THROUGH THE OTHER TEAM'S GOAL POST. SAFETY-2 POINTS. OCCURS WHEN A PLAYER WITH THE BALL IS TACKLED IN HIS OWN END ZONE.

GOAL POST

END ZONE

ICE HOCKEY

Ice hockey's fast skating, rough checking, lightning-fast slapshots, and acrobatic saves make it an exciting sport. Ice hockey, an offshoot of field hockey, began in Canada in the 1800s.

At the end of every National League Hockey season, a silver trophy—the Stanley Cup—is awarded to the team that wins the championship game.

LEARN ABOUT ICE HOCKEY AS YOU LOOK FOR THESE FUN ITEMS:

❑ Baby's block	❑ Clown	❑ Heart	❑ Paper airplane	❑ Skunk
❑ Basketball	❑ Crown	❑ Hot dog	❑ Pencil	❑ Snowman
❑ Blackboard	❑ Feather	❑ Mouse	❑ Periscope	❑ Teapot
❑ Cactus	❑ Flower	❑ Paintbrush	❑ Ski	

What is a hat trick?
How many pro teams are there?

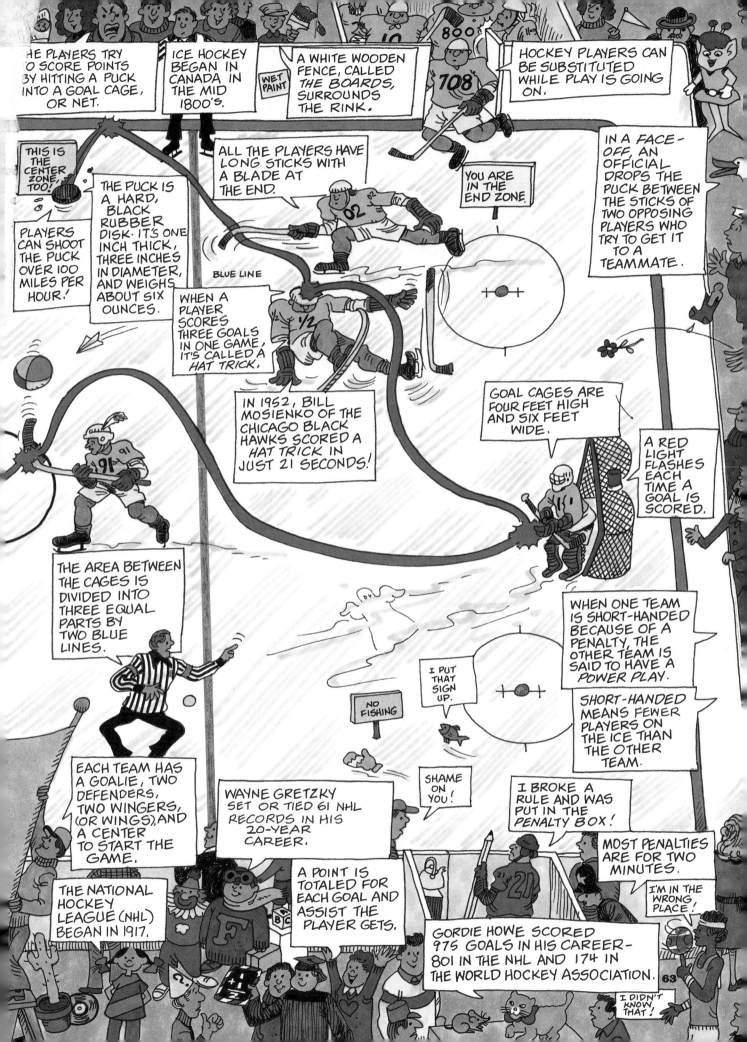

THE PLAYERS TRY TO SCORE POINTS BY HITTING A PUCK INTO A GOAL CAGE, OR NET.

ICE HOCKEY BEGAN IN CANADA IN THE MID 1800'S.

WET PAINT

A WHITE WOODEN FENCE, CALLED THE BOARDS, SURROUNDS THE RINK.

HOCKEY PLAYERS CAN BE SUBSTITUTED WHILE PLAY IS GOING ON.

THIS IS THE CENTER ZONE, TOO!

ALL THE PLAYERS HAVE LONG STICKS WITH A BLADE AT THE END.

YOU ARE IN THE END ZONE.

IN A FACE-OFF, AN OFFICIAL DROPS THE PUCK BETWEEN THE STICKS OF TWO OPPOSING PLAYERS WHO TRY TO GET IT TO A TEAMMATE.

THE PUCK IS A HARD, BLACK RUBBER DISK. IT'S ONE INCH THICK, THREE INCHES IN DIAMETER, AND WEIGHS ABOUT SIX OUNCES.

PLAYERS CAN SHOOT THE PUCK OVER 100 MILES PER HOUR!

BLUE LINE

WHEN A PLAYER SCORES THREE GOALS IN ONE GAME, IT'S CALLED A HAT TRICK.

IN 1952, BILL MOSIENKO OF THE CHICAGO BLACK HAWKS SCORED A HAT TRICK IN JUST 21 SECONDS!

GOAL CAGES ARE FOUR FEET HIGH AND SIX FEET WIDE.

A RED LIGHT FLASHES EACH TIME A GOAL IS SCORED.

THE AREA BETWEEN THE CAGES IS DIVIDED INTO THREE EQUAL PARTS BY TWO BLUE LINES.

WHEN ONE TEAM IS SHORT-HANDED BECAUSE OF A PENALTY, THE OTHER TEAM IS SAID TO HAVE A POWER PLAY.

SHORT-HANDED MEANS FEWER PLAYERS ON THE ICE THAN THE OTHER TEAM.

I PUT THAT SIGN UP.

NO FISHING

SHAME ON YOU!

I BROKE A RULE AND WAS PUT IN THE PENALTY BOX!

EACH TEAM HAS A GOALIE, TWO DEFENDERS, TWO WINGERS, (OR WINGS), AND A CENTER TO START THE GAME.

WAYNE GRETZKY SET OR TIED 61 NHL RECORDS IN HIS 20-YEAR CAREER.

MOST PENALTIES ARE FOR TWO MINUTES.

I'M IN THE WRONG PLACE!

THE NATIONAL HOCKEY LEAGUE (NHL) BEGAN IN 1917.

A POINT IS TOTALED FOR EACH GOAL AND ASSIST THE PLAYER GETS.

GORDIE HOWE SCORED 975 GOALS IN HIS CAREER— 801 IN THE NHL AND 174 IN THE WORLD HOCKEY ASSOCIATION.

I DIDN'T KNOW THAT!

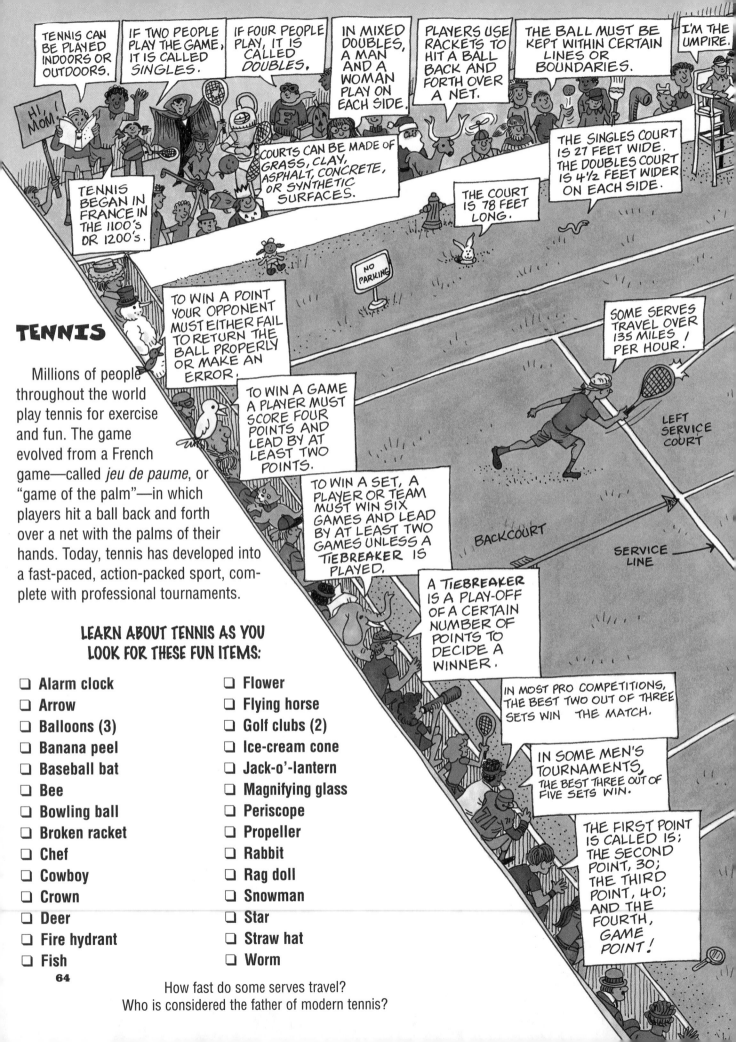

TENNIS

Millions of people throughout the world play tennis for exercise and fun. The game evolved from a French game—called *jeu de paume*, or "game of the palm"—in which players hit a ball back and forth over a net with the palms of their hands. Today, tennis has developed into a fast-paced, action-packed sport, complete with professional tournaments.

LEARN ABOUT TENNIS AS YOU LOOK FOR THESE FUN ITEMS:

- ❑ Alarm clock
- ❑ Arrow
- ❑ Balloons (3)
- ❑ Banana peel
- ❑ Baseball bat
- ❑ Bee
- ❑ Bowling ball
- ❑ Broken racket
- ❑ Chef
- ❑ Cowboy
- ❑ Crown
- ❑ Deer
- ❑ Fire hydrant
- ❑ Fish
- ❑ Flower
- ❑ Flying horse
- ❑ Golf clubs (2)
- ❑ Ice-cream cone
- ❑ Jack-o'-lantern
- ❑ Magnifying glass
- ❑ Periscope
- ❑ Propeller
- ❑ Rabbit
- ❑ Rag doll
- ❑ Snowman
- ❑ Star
- ❑ Straw hat
- ❑ Worm

How fast do some serves travel?
Who is considered the father of modern tennis?

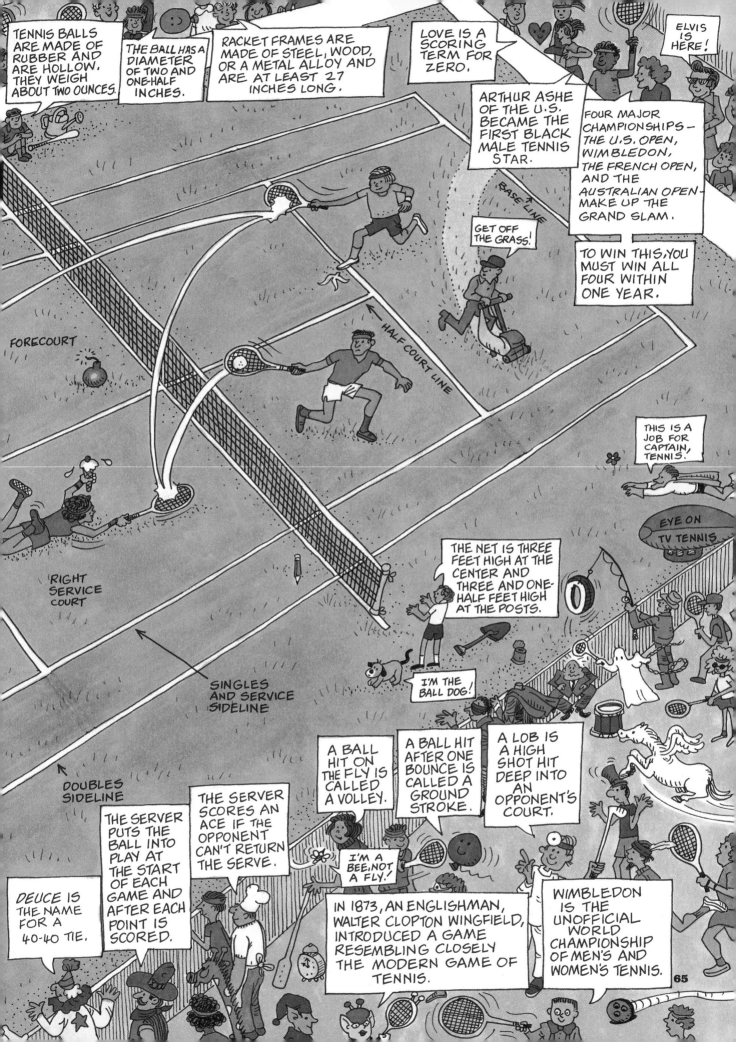

TENNIS BALLS ARE MADE OF RUBBER AND ARE HOLLOW. THEY WEIGH ABOUT TWO OUNCES.

THE BALL HAS A DIAMETER OF TWO AND ONE-HALF INCHES.

RACKET FRAMES ARE MADE OF STEEL, WOOD, OR A METAL ALLOY AND ARE AT LEAST 27 INCHES LONG.

LOVE IS A SCORING TERM FOR ZERO.

ELVIS IS HERE!

ARTHUR ASHE OF THE U.S. BECAME THE FIRST BLACK MALE TENNIS STAR.

FOUR MAJOR CHAMPIONSHIPS— THE U.S. OPEN, WIMBLEDON, THE FRENCH OPEN, AND THE AUSTRALIAN OPEN— MAKE UP THE GRAND SLAM.

GET OFF THE GRASS!

BASE LINE

TO WIN THIS, YOU MUST WIN ALL FOUR WITHIN ONE YEAR.

FORECOURT

HALF COURT LINE

THIS IS A JOB FOR CAPTAIN, TENNIS.

RIGHT SERVICE COURT

EYE ON TV TENNIS

THE NET IS THREE FEET HIGH AT THE CENTER AND THREE AND ONE-HALF FEET HIGH AT THE POSTS.

I'M THE BALL DOG!

SINGLES AND SERVICE SIDELINE

DOUBLES SIDELINE

THE SERVER PUTS THE BALL INTO PLAY AT THE START OF EACH GAME AND AFTER EACH POINT IS SCORED.

THE SERVER SCORES AN ACE IF THE OPPONENT CAN'T RETURN THE SERVE.

A BALL HIT ON THE FLY IS CALLED A VOLLEY.

A BALL HIT AFTER ONE BOUNCE IS CALLED A GROUND STROKE.

A LOB IS A HIGH SHOT HIT DEEP INTO AN OPPONENT'S COURT.

I'M A BEE, NOT A FLY!

DEUCE IS THE NAME FOR A 40-40 TIE.

IN 1873, AN ENGLISHMAN, WALTER CLOPTON WINGFIELD, INTRODUCED A GAME RESEMBLING CLOSELY THE MODERN GAME OF TENNIS.

WIMBLEDON IS THE UNOFFICIAL WORLD CHAMPIONSHIP OF MEN'S AND WOMEN'S TENNIS.

65

MARTIAL ARTS

The martial arts are more than a method of combat. They are important as a means of developing one's physical, spiritual, and mental well-being.

Centuries ago, Buddhist monks roamed throughout Asia, spreading their philosophy and knowledge of the martial arts. Each culture modified this philosophy to suit its needs, thus developing new martial arts techniques.

LEARN ABOUT MARTIAL ARTS AS YOU LOOK FOR THESE FUN ITEMS:

- ❑ Anchor
- ❑ Artist
- ❑ Banana peel
- ❑ Bird
- ❑ Black-belt ghost
- ❑ Bone
- ❑ Book
- ❑ Book of matches
- ❑ Boxer
- ❑ Carrot
- ❑ Chef's hat
- ❑ Clown
- ❑ Crown
- ❑ Football
- ❑ Jack-o'-lantern
- ❑ Karate rat
- ❑ Lost boot
- ❑ Lost glove
- ❑ Lost mitten
- ❑ Magnet
- ❑ Mummy
- ❑ Piggy bank
- ❑ Saw
- ❑ Scarecrow
- ❑ Skateboard
- ❑ Snake
- ❑ Speaker
- ❑ Stopwatch
- ❑ Wizard
- ❑ Yo-yo

What is tae kwon do? How do karate students toughen their hands and feet?

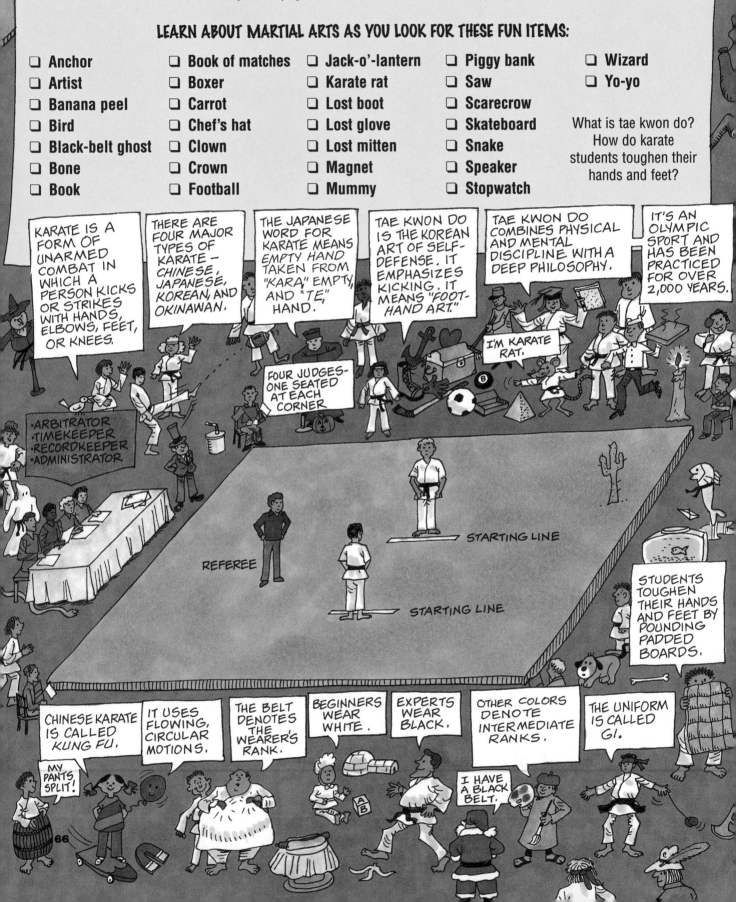

66

WHEN KARATE STUDENTS PRACTICE THEY STOP SHORT OF HITTING THEIR OPPONENT, OR TOUCH THEM LIGHTLY. THIS AVOIDS SERIOUS INJURY.

A DACHI IS A STANCE OR WAY OF STANDING.

THERE ARE DIFFERENT KINDS OF STANCES...

THE READY STANCE, THE CAT STANCE, THE BACK STANCE, THE SIDE STANCE, THE FORWARD STANCE, AND THE HORSEBACK-RIDING STANCE.

THIS IS A FRONT STANCE.

KICKING TECHNIQUES INCLUDE THE HOOK KICK, THE FRONT KICK, THE SIDE KICK, AND THE ROUNDHOUSE KICK.

ONE STRIKES WITH FULL FORCE ONLY IN SELF-DEFENSE.

THIS IS A KNIFE HAND BLOCK.

FLYING FRONT KICK

YOU PUNCH WITH THE KNUCKLES OF THE FIRST TWO FINGERS.

SOUND PLAYS AN IMPORTANT ROLE IN KARATE. WHEN AN ATTACKER STRIKES, YELLING "YAH!" OR "YIAH!" TO PUT MAXIMUM FORCE INTO THE BLOW.

SIDE KICK

STRIKING USES OTHER PARTS OF THE HAND.

ROUNDHOUSE KICKS

A POWER SHOUT IS KNOWN AS A KIYA.

I GET A KICK OUT OF THIS.

I WANT A PEANUT BUTTER SANDWICH!

RIGHT AWAY!

I DIDN'T KNOW THAT!

A SENSEI IS A KARATE TEACHER.
A ZUKI IS A PUNCH.
A UKE IS A BLOCK.
A GERI IS A KICK.
A DOJO IS A KARATE TRAINING HALL.

NOW I KNOW IT!

CRUNCH!

THROUGH THEIR MOVIES, BRUCE LEE AND JACKIE CHAN MADE MARTIAL ARTS POPULAR WORLDWIDE.

I FORGOT MY SHOES.

I'M KARATE TURTLE.

I'M NINJA BUNNY.

TRAINING ENDS WITH A RITSU REI OR STANDING BOW. THIS SHOWS RESPECT TO THE OPPONENT OR TEACHER.

ME TOO!

JAPANESE AIKIDO IS A NON-COMPETITIVE MARTIAL ART.

A MATCH USUALLY LASTS TWO MINUTES.

THREE POINTS USUALLY WINS A MATCH. IF NO ONE HAS SCORED THREE POINTS, THE ONE WITH THE MOST POINTS WINS.

A KATA COMPETITION USES A PREARRANGED SEQUENCE OF KICKS, BLOCKS, AND PUNCHES TO DEMONSTRATE SKILL.

YOU BROKE THE BOARD!

THEY DON'T NEED ME!

67

TRACK AND FIELD

Track and field is a sport in which men and women compete in athletic events that feature running, throwing, and jumping. Track events consist of a series of races over various distances, ranging from 60 meters (65.6 yards) to a marathon. Field events measure an athlete's ability to throw or jump.

LEARN ABOUT TRACK AND FIELD AS YOU LOOK FOR THESE FUN ITEMS:

- ☐ Balloon
- ☐ Bee
- ☐ Birdcage
- ☐ Chef's hat
- ☐ Count Dracula
- ☐ Duck
- ☐ Elephant
- ☐ Fish
- ☐ Flying bat
- ☐ Football player

- ☐ Helicopter
- ☐ Ice-cream cone
- ☐ Mummy
- ☐ Ostrich

- ☐ Painted egg
- ☐ Periscope
- ☐ Pig
- ☐ Pizza deliveryman
- ☐ Rabbit
- ☐ Roller skater

- ☐ Surfboard
- ☐ Tuba
- ☐ Turtle
- ☐ Umbrella

How long is a marathon?
Name the four throwing events.

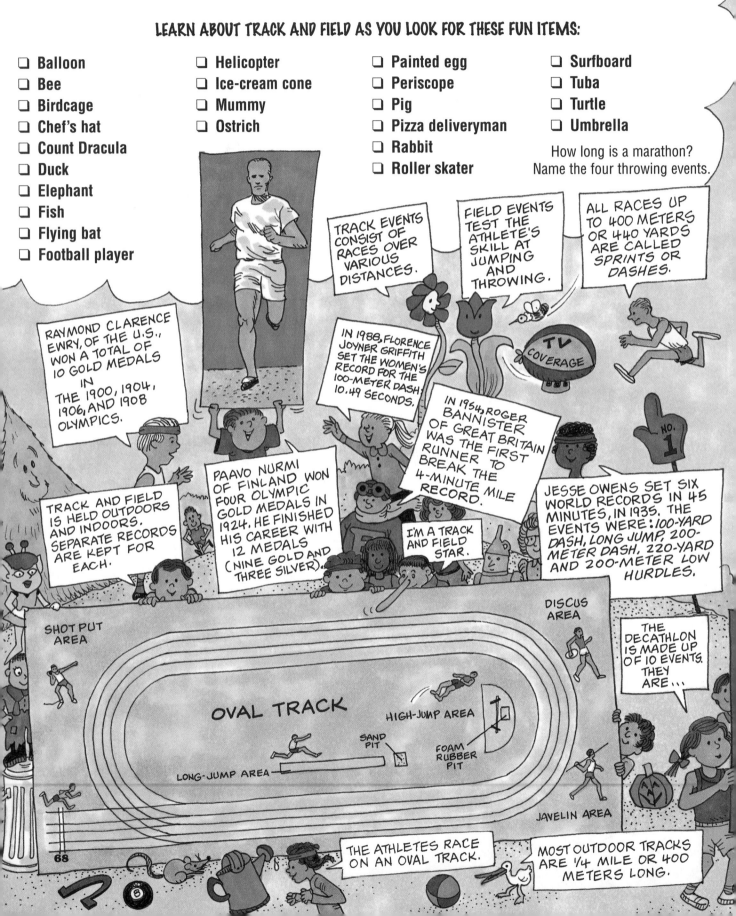

TRACK EVENTS CONSIST OF RACES OVER VARIOUS DISTANCES.

FIELD EVENTS TEST THE ATHLETE'S SKILL AT JUMPING AND THROWING.

ALL RACES UP TO 400 METERS OR 440 YARDS ARE CALLED SPRINTS OR DASHES.

RAYMOND CLARENCE EWRY, OF THE U.S., WON A TOTAL OF 10 GOLD MEDALS IN THE 1900, 1904, 1906, AND 1908 OLYMPICS.

IN 1988, FLORENCE JOYNER GRIFFITH SET THE WOMEN'S RECORD FOR THE 100-METER DASH: 10.49 SECONDS.

IN 1954, ROGER BANNISTER OF GREAT BRITAIN WAS THE FIRST RUNNER TO BREAK THE 4-MINUTE MILE RECORD.

TV COVERAGE

TRACK AND FIELD IS HELD OUTDOORS AND INDOORS. SEPARATE RECORDS ARE KEPT FOR EACH.

PAAVO NURMI OF FINLAND WON FOUR OLYMPIC GOLD MEDALS IN 1924. HE FINISHED HIS CAREER WITH 12 MEDALS (NINE GOLD AND THREE SILVER).

I'M A TRACK AND FIELD STAR.

JESSE OWENS SET SIX WORLD RECORDS IN 45 MINUTES, IN 1935. THE EVENTS WERE: 100-YARD DASH, LONG JUMP, 200-METER DASH, 220-YARD AND 200-METER LOW HURDLES.

NO. 1

DISCUS AREA

SHOT PUT AREA

THE DECATHLON IS MADE UP OF 10 EVENTS. THEY ARE...

OVAL TRACK

HIGH-JUMP AREA

LONG-JUMP AREA

SAND PIT

FOAM RUBBER PIT

JAVELIN AREA

THE ATHLETES RACE ON AN OVAL TRACK.

MOST OUTDOOR TRACKS ARE 1/4 MILE OR 400 METERS LONG.

EXTREME SPORTS

What's more fun than taking action to the edge? "Nothing!" say extreme-sports fans.

LEARN ABOUT BMX AS YOU LOOK FOR THESE FUN ITEMS:

- ☐ Brush
- ☐ Flower
- ☐ Football
- ☐ Key
- ☐ Paintbrush
- ☐ Snail
- ☐ Star
- ☐ Worms (2)

MOTOCROSS GAINED POPULARITY IN THE LATE 1940'S.

IN THE EARLY 1970 S, KIDS AROUND THE U.S.A. WOULD SET UP HILLY, BUMPY MOTOCROSS TRAILS AND RACE ON THEM WITH THEIR BICYCLES. THIS WAS THE START OF BMX (BICYCLE MOTOCROSS).

RIDERS RACE THEIR MOTORCYCLES OVER BUMPY, TWISTY TERRAIN.

ALL BMXERS WEAR PROTECTIVE GEAR: HELMET, GOGGLES, GLOVES, LONG SLEEVES, AND PANTS.

EVEN BMX BIKES HAVE TO BE PADDED!

LEARN ABOUT SNOW-BOARDING AS YOU LOOK FOR THESE FUN ITEMS:

- ☐ Baseball cap
- ☐ Birds (2)
- ☐ Cactus
- ☐ Heart
- ☐ Lost cap
- ☐ Rabbit
- ☐ Sled
- ☐ Star
- ☐ Sunglasses

THE FIRST SNOWBOARD WAS INVENTED IN 1964 BY SHERMAN POPPEN.

AT FIRST RIDERS HAD TO COMPETE FOR SPACE ON SKI SLOPES OR IN STEEP FOREST AREAS.

IN THE EARLY 1980 S, THE SPORT BECAME KNOWN AS SNOWBOARDING.

POPPEN BOLTED TWO SKIS TOGETHER FOR HIS DAUGHTER, WENDY, TO RIDE ON. IT WAS CALLED A SNURFER (COMBINING SNOW AND SURF).

THE SNURFER GAINED TREMENDOUS POPULARITY IN THE 1970 S, ESPECIALLY WITH SKATEBOARDERS AND SURFERS.

1981 SAW THE FIRST SNOWBOARDING COMPETITION IN LEADVILLE, COLORADO.

WOW!

LEARN ABOUT SKATEBOARDING AS YOU LOOK FOR THESE FUN ITEMS:

- ☐ Balloons
- ☐ Elephant
- ☐ Half moon
- ☐ Kite
- ☐ Lightning bolts (2)
- ☐ Stars (3)
- ☐ Top hat

What does BMX stand for?
Who invented the snowboard?
What is an Ollie?

SKATEBOARDING WAS BORN IN THE 1930 S AND 1940 S, WHEN KIDS ATTACHED ROLLER SKATES TO PLANKS OF WOOD.

LOOKS LIKE FUN TO ME!

SURFERS FROM ALL AROUND GOT HOOKED ON STREET SURFING.

IN 1958, CALIFORNIA SURFER BILL RICHARDS MADE SKATEBOARDS FOR WHEN THE WAVES WERE TOO SMALL TO SURF.

THE FIRST NATIONAL SKATEBOARD CHAMPIONSHIP WAS HELD IN CALIFORNIA, IN 1965.

RIDING "FAKIE" MEANS RIDING BACKWARDS.

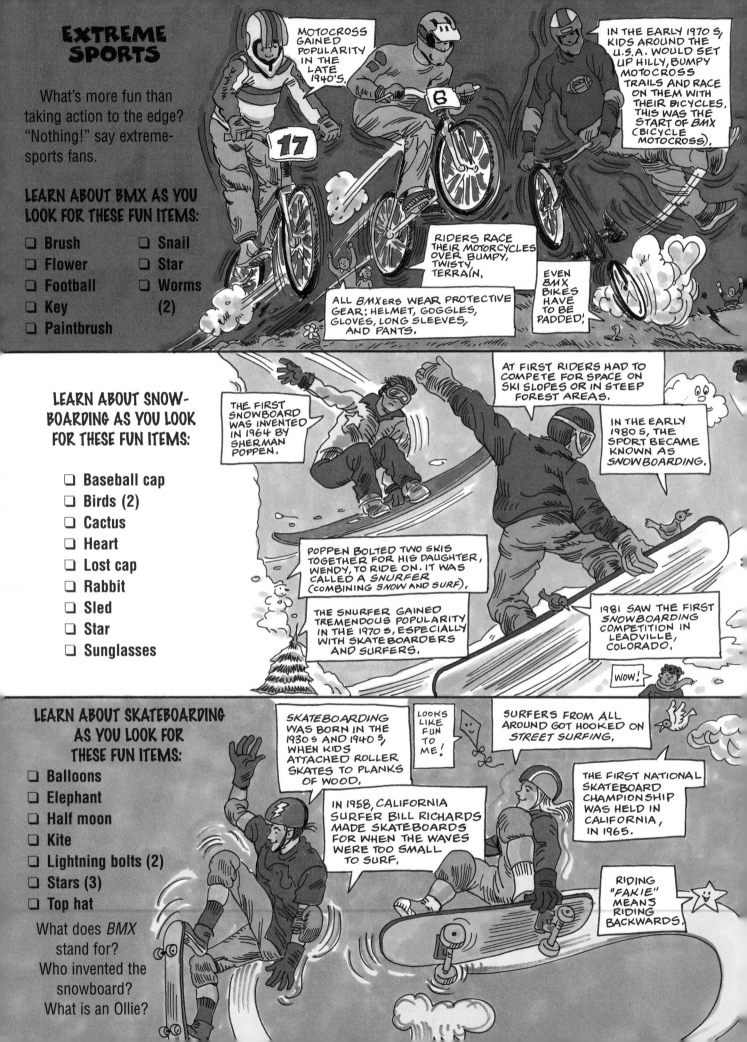

WHEN RIDERS CATCH AIR, THEY DO FANTASTIC TRICKS!

BMX COURSES ARE SET UP OVER DIRT AND ROCK TERRAIN.

THE KEY TO WINNING A RACE IS TO MOVE QUICKLY AND SMOOTHLY THROUGH THE COURSE.

THERE ARE DOUBLE AND TRIPLE HILLS, BANKED AND FLAT CURVES, AND LOTS OF BUMPS.

BMX LEGEND DAVE CLINTON WAS THE FIRST TO BE INDUCTED INTO THE AMERICAN BICYCLE ASSOCIATION (ABA) HALL OF FAME, IN 1985.

THE ABA HALL OF FAME IS IN GILBERT, ARIZONA.

THE FIRST SNOWBOARDING WORLD CHAMPIONSHIPS WERE ORGANIZED BY SNOWBOARD DEVELOPER TOM SIMS.

THEY WERE HELD IN SODA SPRINGS, CALIFORNIA, IN 1983.

SNOWBOARDING MADE ITS OLYMPIC DEBUT IN THE 1998 WINTER GAMES AT NAGANO, JAPAN.

THERE ARE TWO SNOWBOARDING EVENTS IN THE OLYMPICS: HALFPIPE, WHERE RIDERS EARN POINTS FOR THEIR STYLE, SKILL, AND AIR TIME; GIANT SLALOM, WHERE RIDERS ARE TIMED AS THEY MAKE THEIR WAY DOWN A STEEP SLALOM COURSE.

IN 1990, VAIL SKI RESORT IN COLORADO WAS THE FIRST TO OPEN A SEPARATE SECTION FOR SNOWBOARDING.

IF A RIDER CATCHES TOO MUCH AIR AND LOSES CONTROL, IT'S CALLED "ROLLIN' DOWN THE WINDOWS," BECAUSE USUALLY HER ARMS WILL BE CIRCLING LIKE SHE'S ROLLING DOWN THE WINDOWS IN A CAR.

SHAWN PALMER, TERJE HAAKONSEN, AND ROSS POWERS ARE SOME OF SNOWBOARDING'S SUPERSTARS AND LEGENDS.

IN 1971, THE KICKTAIL WAS ADDED TO THE SKATEBOARD AND ITS POPULARITY SOARED.

IN THE LATE 1970 S, ALAN "OLLIE" GELFAND WAS THE FIRST TO TIP THE TAIL OF THE BOARD DOWN AND JUMP INTO THE AIR.

THAT JUMP MOVE IS CALLED AN OLLIE, AND WAS THE FIRST OF THOUSANDS OF SKATEBOARD TRICKS TO COME.

FAMOUS DANCER AND MOVIE STAR FRED ASTAIRE EVEN HAD A SKATEBOARD.

AN OLLIE IS WHEN YOU JUMP UP AND CATCH AIR WITH YOUR BOARD.

BY THE LATE 1990 S, MORE THAN 6 MILLION AMERICANS WERE SKATEBOARDING. ALMOST HALF OF THEM LIVED IN CALIFORNIA.

FAMOUS PEOPLE AND PLACES

WALT DISNEY WORLD

Walt Disney World is the fulfillment of Walt Disney's dream. He wanted to create the ultimate amusement park, which adults and children could enjoy together. Today, Walt Disney World in Florida is the most popular man-made attraction in the world, visited by thousands of people each day.

LEARN ABOUT WALT DISNEY WORLD AS YOU LOOK FOR THESE FUN ITEMS:

- ❑ Arrow
- ❑ Balloon
- ❑ Cake
- ❑ Chef's hat
- ❑ Clown
- ❑ Elephants (2)
- ❑ Fish
- ❑ Football
- ❑ Ghost
- ❑ Hearts (3)
- ❑ Horse
- ❑ Ice-cream cone
- ❑ Kite
- ❑ Ladder
- ❑ Magnifying glass
- ❑ Penguin
- ❑ Snowman
- ❑ TV set

Who starred in *Steamboat Willie*?
On what day is Walt Disney World busiest?

SACAGAWEA

Sacagawea *(SAK-uh-juh-WEE-uh)* was born among the Shoshone *(shoh-SHOH-nee)* Indians. As a young girl, she was captured by an enemy tribe, then sold as a slave to a French-Canadian trader, who later married her. Sacagawea and her husband both joined the expedition led by Meriwether Lewis and William Clark in 1804-1805. Sacagawea served as interpreter and guide as the team crossed western lands to the Pacific Ocean, then back again.

LEARN ABOUT SACAGAWEA AS YOU LOOK FOR THESE FUN ITEMS:

- ❑ Armadillo
- ❑ Arrows (2)
- ❑ Bears (2)
- ❑ Beaver
- ❑ Bow
- ❑ Buffalo
- ❑ Deer
- ❑ Drum
- ❑ Eagle
- ❑ Egg
- ❑ Flying bat
- ❑ Flying saucer
- ❑ Frog
- ❑ Groundhog
- ❑ Heart
- ❑ Lost boot
- ❑ Moose
- ❑ Mushroom
- ❑ Owl
- ❑ Rabbits (3)
- ❑ Sailboat
- ❑ Skunk
- ❑ Snake
- ❑ Spear
- ❑ Wild turkey

What does *Sacagawea* mean? Why did she agree to guide Lewis and Clark?

SHE HELPED THE U.S. GAIN THE LAND THAT IS NOW THE STATES OF WASHINGTON, OREGON, IDAHO, MONTANA, AND WYOMING!

KEEP OUR WILDERNESS CLEAN

YOU ARE HERE ✗

SINCE 2000, U.S. DOLLAR COINS HAVE FEATURED A PICTURE OF SACAGAWEA AND HER INFANT SON.

I'M A ROCKY MOUNTAIN GOAT.

THEY'LL REACH THE PACIFIC OCEAN IN NOVEMBER, 1805.

SACAGAWEA'S NAME MEANS "BIRD WOMAN."

THAT'S A NICE NAME.

I WANT TO SEE THAT!

THEY'LL NAME A RIVER, A MOUNTAIN PEAK, AND A MOUNTAIN PASS AFTER HER!

WELCOME! MY SISTER!

THIS IS THE HOME WHERE I ROAM.

CAMEAHWAIT IS MY BROTHER, CHIEF OF THE SHOSHONE TRIBE.

WE HAVE ORDERS FROM PRESIDENT JEFFERSON TO SURVEY THE NORTHWEST TERRITORY!

ARE THEY STAYING FOR DINNER?

A REAL CHIEF!

HE WILL GIVE US SUPPLIES TO CONTINUE OUR JOURNEY.

WE'LL GIVE THE SHOSHONE GIFTS OF KNIVES, POCKET MIRRORS, SILK RIBBONS, AND SEWING NEEDLES.

I LIKE TO PLAY THE DRUMS.

WEST

I'M A GO-FOR.

I'M A GOPHER.

WHAT'S THE CONTINENTAL DIVIDE?

IT'S THE RIDGE OF THE ROCKY MOUNTAINS WHICH SEPARATES RIVERS FLOWING IN AN EASTERLY DIRECTION FROM THOSE FLOWING IN A WESTERLY DIRECTION.

SHE WAS BORN IN THE ROCKY MOUNTAINS OF IDAHO!

HOW ABOUT GIVING ME SOME CARROTS?

I'M A GROUND-HOG. DO YOU SEE MY SHADOW?

HE'S A WISE OLD OWL.

I DIDN'T KNOW THAT!

I'M AN ARMADILLO.

SOME SAY SACAGAWEA LIVED TO BE 100 YEARS OLD.

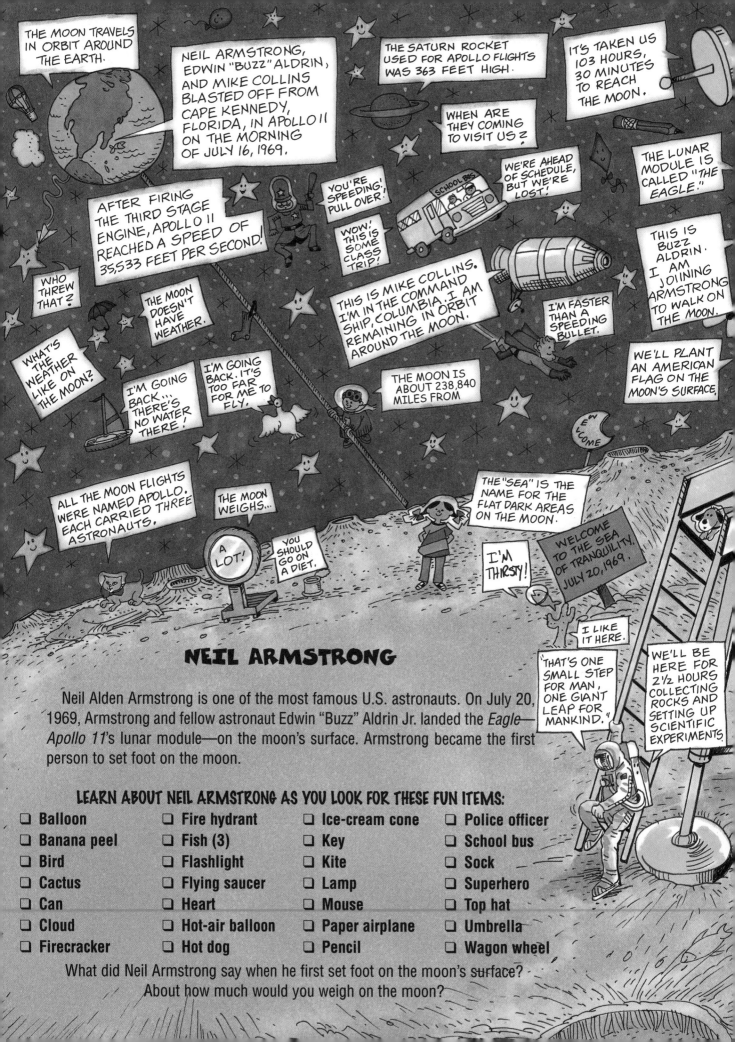

NEIL ARMSTRONG

Neil Alden Armstrong is one of the most famous U.S. astronauts. On July 20, 1969, Armstrong and fellow astronaut Edwin "Buzz" Aldrin Jr. landed the *Eagle*—*Apollo 11*'s lunar module—on the moon's surface. Armstrong became the first person to set foot on the moon.

LEARN ABOUT NEIL ARMSTRONG AS YOU LOOK FOR THESE FUN ITEMS:

- ☐ Balloon
- ☐ Banana peel
- ☐ Bird
- ☐ Cactus
- ☐ Can
- ☐ Cloud
- ☐ Firecracker
- ☐ Fire hydrant
- ☐ Fish (3)
- ☐ Flashlight
- ☐ Flying saucer
- ☐ Heart
- ☐ Hot-air balloon
- ☐ Hot dog
- ☐ Ice-cream cone
- ☐ Key
- ☐ Kite
- ☐ Lamp
- ☐ Mouse
- ☐ Paper airplane
- ☐ Pencil
- ☐ Police officer
- ☐ School bus
- ☐ Sock
- ☐ Superhero
- ☐ Top hat
- ☐ Umbrella
- ☐ Wagon wheel

What did Neil Armstrong say when he first set foot on the moon's surface?
About how much would you weigh on the moon?

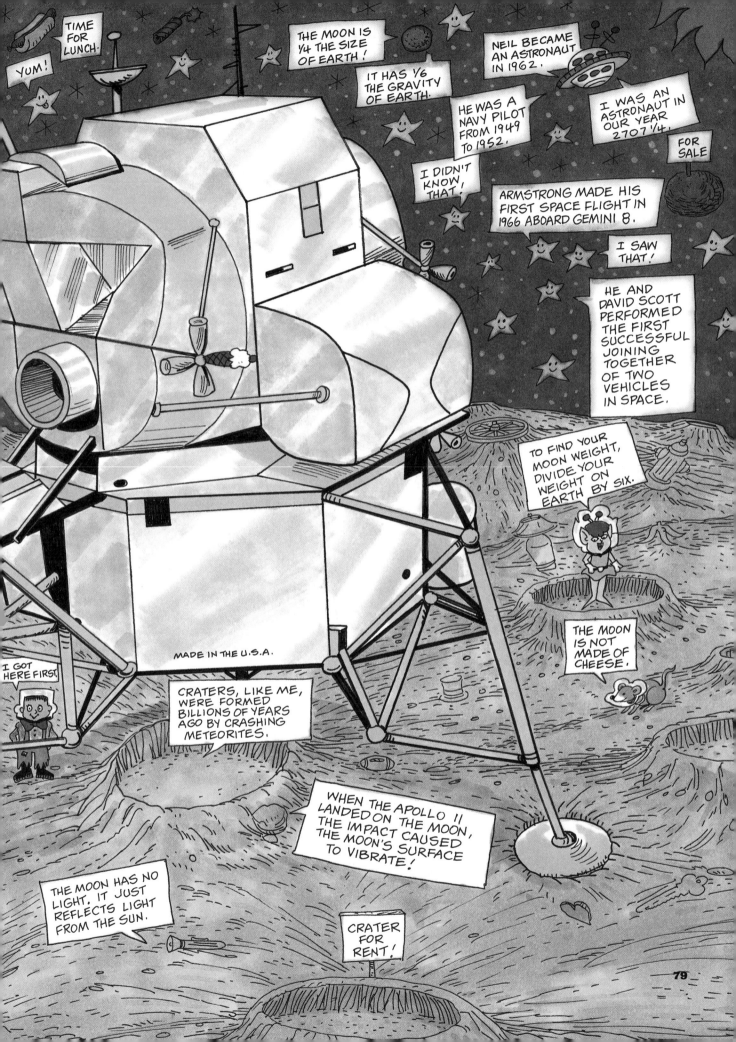

WASHINGTON, D.C.

George Washington envisioned a city of beauty and stature to serve as the nation's capital. In 1791, he hired Pierre L'Enfant—a French architect and engineer—to design it. L'Enfant's plan served Washington's dream well. The city has wide, straight avenues; lush parks; towering monuments; and beautiful trees and flowers. It also is an important political center, where decisions affecting millions of lives are made daily at the White House (home of the president), the Capitol (home of the U.S. Congress), the Supreme Court, and many federal agencies.

LEARN ABOUT WASHINGTON, D.C., AS YOU LOOK FOR THESE FUN ITEMS:

- ❏ Balloon
- ❏ Baseball cap
- ❏ Bird
- ❏ Cactus
- ❏ Fish
- ❏ Fishbowl
- ❏ Flags (3)
- ❏ Flower
- ❏ Headband
- ❏ Key
- ❏ Kite
- ❏ Mouse
- ❏ Paintbrush
- ❏ Scarves (2)
- ❏ Star
- ❏ Top hat
- ❏ Turtle

What is this city's purpose?

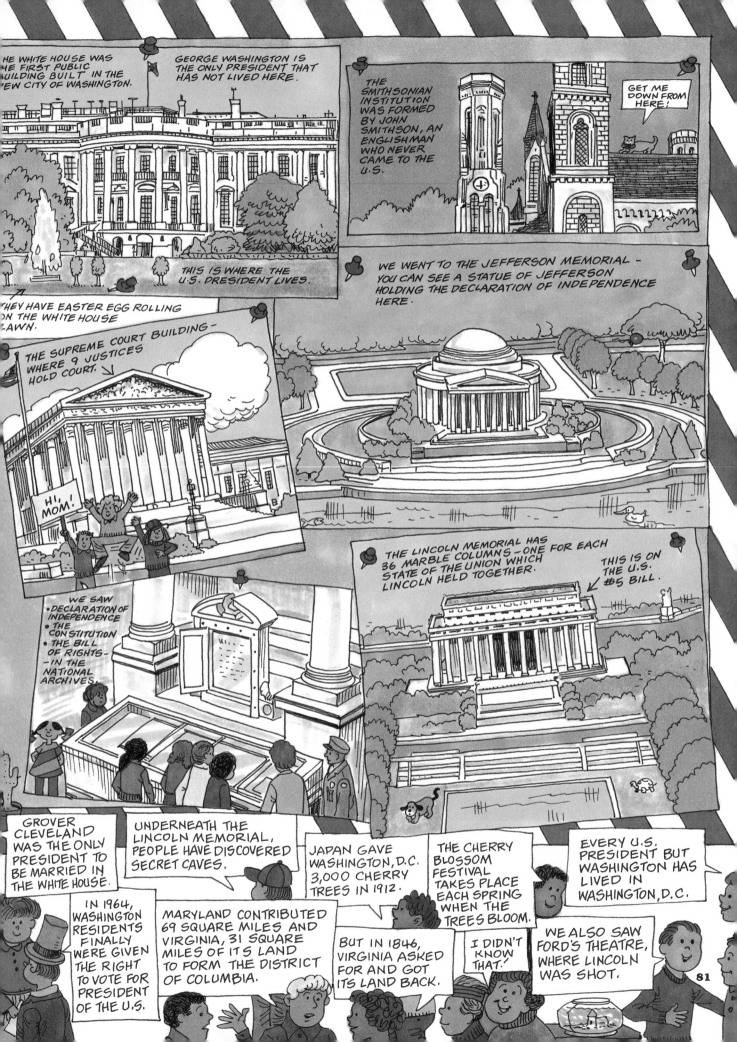

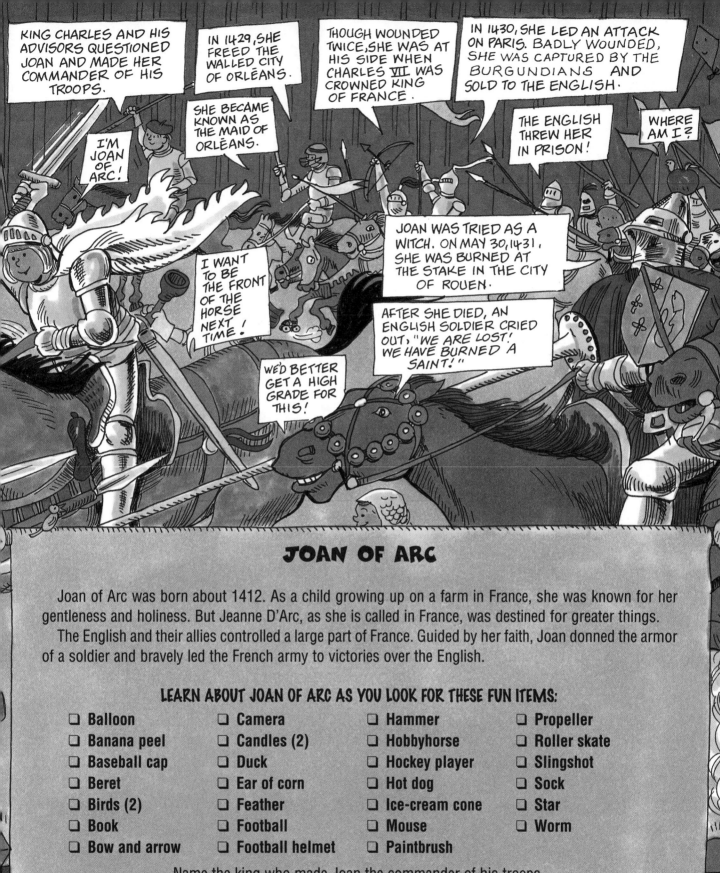

JOAN OF ARC

Joan of Arc was born about 1412. As a child growing up on a farm in France, she was known for her gentleness and holiness. But Jeanne D'Arc, as she is called in France, was destined for greater things.

The English and their allies controlled a large part of France. Guided by her faith, Joan donned the armor of a soldier and bravely led the French army to victories over the English.

LEARN ABOUT JOAN OF ARC AS YOU LOOK FOR THESE FUN ITEMS:

- ❑ Balloon
- ❑ Banana peel
- ❑ Baseball cap
- ❑ Beret
- ❑ Birds (2)
- ❑ Book
- ❑ Bow and arrow

- ❑ Camera
- ❑ Candles (2)
- ❑ Duck
- ❑ Ear of corn
- ❑ Feather
- ❑ Football
- ❑ Football helmet

- ❑ Hammer
- ❑ Hobbyhorse
- ❑ Hockey player
- ❑ Hot dog
- ❑ Ice-cream cone
- ❑ Mouse
- ❑ Paintbrush

- ❑ Propeller
- ❑ Roller skate
- ❑ Slingshot
- ❑ Sock
- ❑ Star
- ❑ Worm

Name the king who made Joan the commander of his troops.
Where was Joan captured?

JACQUES-YVES COUSTEAU

Jacques-Yves Cousteau made scuba diving and underwater exploration popular by inventing and perfecting the aqualung. Cousteau won many awards for his underwater films, and also wrote many books about sea life. He began the Cousteau Society to preserve the beauty of the ocean life he loved to explore.

LEARN ABOUT JACQUES-YVES COUSTEAU AS YOU LOOK FOR THESE FUN ITEMS:

- ❏ Balloons (3)
- ❏ Bathyscaphe
- ❏ Bottle
- ❏ Bucket
- ❏ Can
- ❏ Duck
- ❏ Hammer
- ❏ Helicopter
- ❏ Horseshoe
- ❏ Horseshoe crab
- ❏ Jellyfish
- ❏ Lifesaver
- ❏ Lost oar
- ❏ Lost shorts
- ❏ Palm tree
- ❏ Paper airplane
- ❏ Pencil
- ❏ Periscope
- ❏ Sailboat
- ❏ Sea horse
- ❏ Shipwreck
- ❏ Shipwrecked sailor
- ❏ Starfish
- ❏ Surfer
- ❏ Swan
- ❏ Telescope
- ❏ Tire
- ❏ TV set
- ❏ Wagon wheel

What was the name of Cousteau's research ship?
What did Cousteau help invent that is used by scuba divers?

NEW YORK CITY

New York City is the most populous city in the United States. It is a universal center for art, fashion, architecture, finance, publishing, and more. A great deal of what happens in New York affects what happens around the country and even around the world.

LEARN ABOUT NEW YORK CITY AS YOU LOOK FOR THESE FUN ITEMS:

- ☐ Apple
- ☐ Baseball
- ☐ Bird
- ☐ Blimp
- ☐ Book
- ☐ Boom box
- ☐ Container ship
- ☐ Diver
- ☐ Ferry
- ☐ Fish

- ☐ Flower
- ☐ Flying saucer
- ☐ Football
- ☐ Ghost
- ☐ Heart
- ☐ Helicopter
- ☐ Periscope

- ☐ Rowboat
- ☐ Star
- ☐ Telescope
- ☐ Tire

- ☐ Top hat
- ☐ Tugboat
- ☐ Worm

Who first settled New York?
When was it the nation's capital?

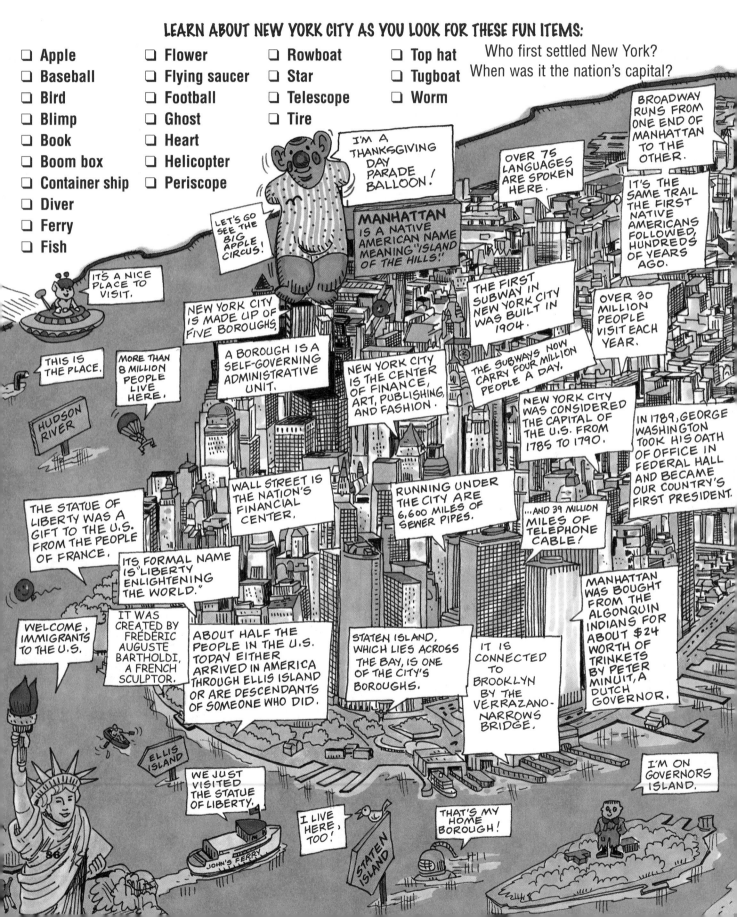

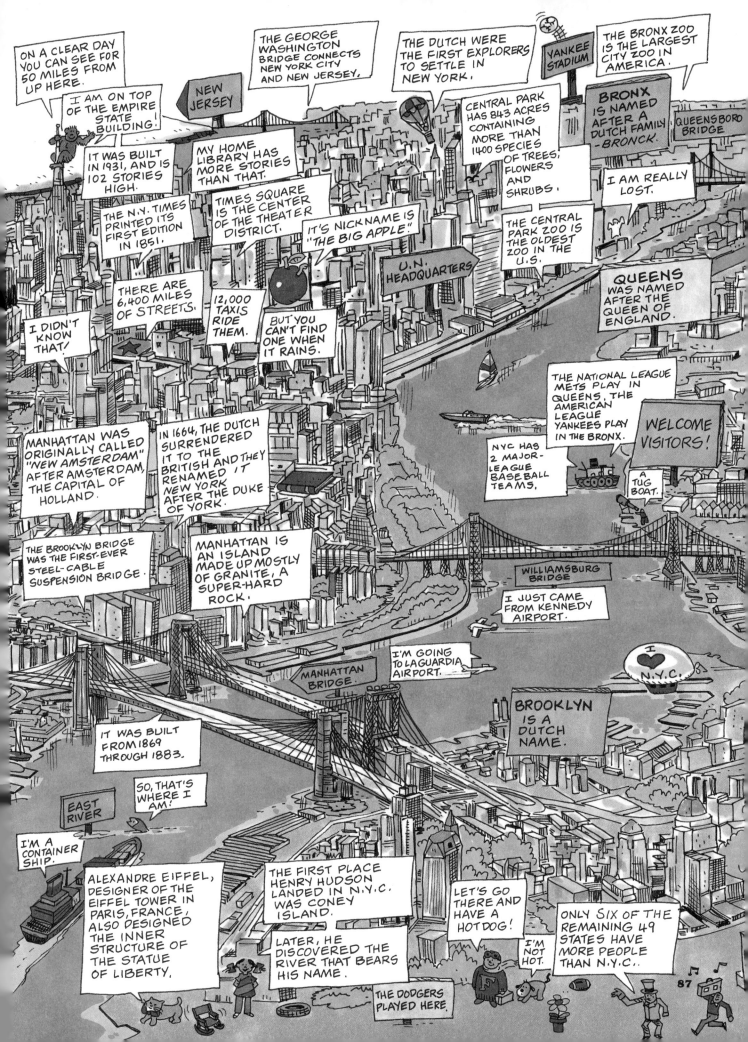

THE PYRAMIDS AND THE GREAT SPHINX

The pyramids of Egypt, built about 5,000 years ago, are the world's oldest stone buildings. Incredibly, these huge structures were built by men without the aid of machinery. Each pyramid was a pharaoh's tomb, and contained all the goods his people believed he would need in his next life.

The Great Sphinx at Giza, Egypt, is one of the world's most recognized monuments.

LEARN ABOUT THE PYRAMIDS AND THE GREAT SPHINX AS YOU LOOK FOR THESE FUN ITEMS:

- ❑ Arrow
- ❑ Bone
- ❑ Camels (2)
- ❑ Cup
- ❑ Elephant
- ❑ Fire hydrant
- ❑ Fish
- ❑ Flying carpet
- ❑ Ghost
- ❑ Golfer
- ❑ Hammer
- ❑ Heart
- ❑ Helmet
- ❑ Horseshoe
- ❑ Jack-o'-lantern
- ❑ Key
- ❑ Mouse
- ❑ Mummy
- ❑ Photographers (3)
- ❑ Sand castle
- ❑ Shovels (2)
- ❑ Sled
- ❑ Snake
- ❑ Star
- ❑ Telescope
- ❑ Tent
- ❑ Trumpet
- ❑ Umbrella

What were the Egyptian kings called?
Why was the Great Sphinx built?

LEONARDO DA VINCI

Leonardo da Vinci (1452–1519) was one of the greatest artists of the Renaissance. However, his interests and accomplishments went far beyond the world of art. He was, at various times, an inventor, scientist, engineer, architect, and designer. Leonardo's investigations marked the beginning of the scientific revolution and paved the way for scientists and inventors who followed him to take their places in history.

LEARN ABOUT LEONARDO DA VINCI AS YOU LOOK FOR THESE FUN ITEMS:

- ❑ Balloon
- ❑ Banana peel
- ❑ Birds (2)
- ❑ Bone
- ❑ Candles (13)
- ❑ Cane
- ❑ Chef
- ❑ Crown
- ❑ Doctor
- ❑ Duck
- ❑ Easel
- ❑ Feather
- ❑ Flowerpot
- ❑ Flying bat
- ❑ Ghost
- ❑ Graduate
- ❑ *La Gioconda*
- ❑ Ladder
- ❑ Lifesaver
- ❑ Lost shoe
- ❑ Mouse
- ❑ Paintbrushes (2)
- ❑ Paint bucket
- ❑ Painted egg
- ❑ Paper airplane
- ❑ Pencil
- ❑ Pizza
- ❑ Screwdriver
- ❑ Skull
- ❑ Snowman
- ❑ Stool
- ❑ Wizard

For what is the *Mona Lisa* famous?
Why must a mirror be used in order to read Leonardo's notebooks?

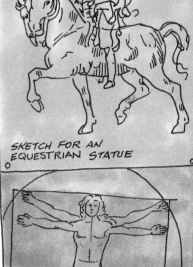

SKETCH FOR AN EQUESTRIAN STATUE

HUMAN PROPORTIONS RECONSTRUCTED ACCORDING TO VITRUVIUS— 1487-90

PLAN FOR A CHURCH— 1487-89

ANATOMY— MUSCLES OF UPPER LIMB

LEONARDO WAS ALSO AN ARCHITECT, MUSICIAN, MATHEMATICIAN, AND SCULPTOR.

HE'S GOING TO PAINT MY PORTRAIT.

"RENAISSANCE" MEANS "REBIRTH."

ANATOMY IS THE STUDY OF THE STRUCTURE OF THE BODY.

HIS ARE THE FIRST ACCURATE DRAWINGS OF ANATOMY.

I'M LOST!

HE MADE MAPS OF EUROPE.

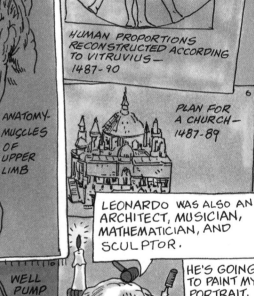

MACHINE FOR MAKING CONCAVE MIRRORS

WELL PUMP

IN 1482, HE BECAME COURT ARTIST FOR THE DUKE OF MILAN.

AS A MILITARY ENGINEER FOR THE DUKE, HE DESIGNED A MOVABLE BRIDGE, DIFFERENT TYPES OF LADDERS FOR STORMING AND CLIMBING CASTLE WALLS, ARTILLERY, AND GUNS.

HIS PAINTINGS ARE GRACEFUL, CALM, AND DELICATE.

HE EXPLORED HUMAN ANATOMY AND PERSPECTIVE.

THE FIRST SUCCESSFUL HELICOPTER, DESIGNED IN THE 1930S, WAS BASED ON LEONARDO'S DRAWINGS.

HE BASED HIS DRAWINGS ON THE ACTION OF A SCREW.

HE HAS GREAT POWERS OF OBSERVATION.

HE RECORDED HIS IDEAS OF ART, SCIENCE, AND ENGINEERING IN NOTEBOOKS.

HE WROTE HIS NOTES BACKWARD SO THEY CAN ONLY BE READ USING A MIRROR.

YOU ARE HERE X

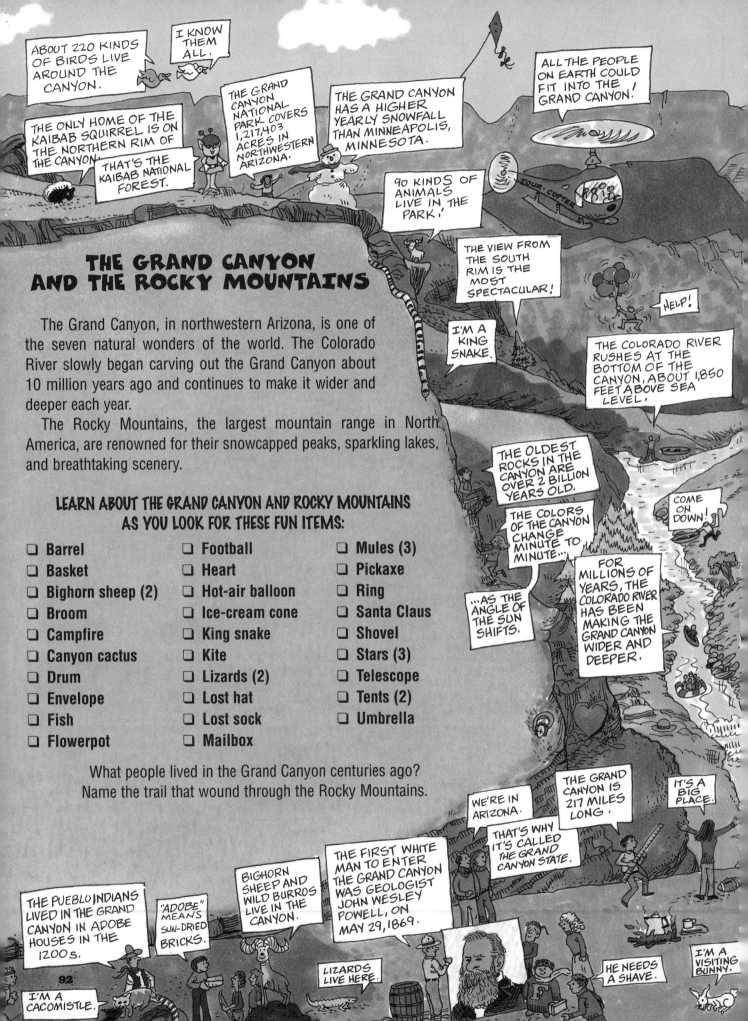

THE GRAND CANYON AND THE ROCKY MOUNTAINS

The Grand Canyon, in northwestern Arizona, is one of the seven natural wonders of the world. The Colorado River slowly began carving out the Grand Canyon about 10 million years ago and continues to make it wider and deeper each year.

The Rocky Mountains, the largest mountain range in North America, are renowned for their snowcapped peaks, sparkling lakes, and breathtaking scenery.

LEARN ABOUT THE GRAND CANYON AND ROCKY MOUNTAINS AS YOU LOOK FOR THESE FUN ITEMS:

- ❏ Barrel
- ❏ Basket
- ❏ Bighorn sheep (2)
- ❏ Broom
- ❏ Campfire
- ❏ Canyon cactus
- ❏ Drum
- ❏ Envelope
- ❏ Fish
- ❏ Flowerpot
- ❏ Football
- ❏ Heart
- ❏ Hot-air balloon
- ❏ Ice-cream cone
- ❏ King snake
- ❏ Kite
- ❏ Lizards (2)
- ❏ Lost hat
- ❏ Lost sock
- ❏ Mailbox
- ❏ Mules (3)
- ❏ Pickaxe
- ❏ Ring
- ❏ Santa Claus
- ❏ Shovel
- ❏ Stars (3)
- ❏ Telescope
- ❏ Tents (2)
- ❏ Umbrella

What people lived in the Grand Canyon centuries ago?
Name the trail that wound through the Rocky Mountains.

92